FINGERS TO THE BONE:
UNITED STATES FAILURE TO PROTECT
CHILD FARMWORKERS

Human Rights Watch
New York · Washington · London · Brussels

ISBN 1-56432-249-1
Library of Congress Catalog Card Number 00-104893

Cover Design by Rafael Jiménez
Cover photo © Paul Kitagaki/The Oregonian
A young farmworker's hands are stained with strawberries and dirt after
a day of picking.

Addresses for Human Rights Watch
350 Fifth Avenue, 34th Floor, New York, NY 10118-3299
Tel: (212) 290-4700, Fax: (212) 736-1300, E-mail: hrwnyc@hrw.org

1630 Connecticut Avenue, N.W., Suite 500, Washington, DC 20009
Tel: (202) 612-4321, Fax: (202) 612-4333, E-mail: hrwdc@hrw.org

33 Islington High Street, N1 9LH London, UK
Tel: (171) 713-1995, Fax: (171) 713-1800, E-mail: hrwatchuk@gn.apc.org

15 Rue Van Campenhout, 1000 Brussels, Belgium
Tel: (2) 732-2009, Fax: (2) 732-0471, E-mail:hrwatcheu@skynet.be

Web Site Address: http://www.hrw.org

Listserv address: To subscribe to the list, send an e-mail message to
majordomo@igc.apc.org with "subscribe hrw-news" in the body of the message
(leave the subject line blank).

Human Rights Watch is dedicated to
protecting the human rights of people around the world.

We stand with victims and activists to prevent
discrimination, to uphold political freedom, to protect people from
inhumane conduct in wartime, and to bring offenders to justice.

We investigate and expose
human rights violations and hold abusers accountable.

We challenge governments and those who hold power to end abusive
practices and respect international human rights law.

We enlist the public and the international
community to support the cause of human rights for all.

HUMAN RIGHTS WATCH

Human Rights Watch conducts regular, systematic investigations of human rights abuses in some seventy countries around the world. Our reputation for timely, reliable disclosures has made us an essential source of information for those concerned with human rights. We address the human rights practices of governments of all political stripes, of all geopolitical alignments, and of all ethnic and religious persuasions. Human Rights Watch defends freedom of thought and expression, due process and equal protection of the law, and a vigorous civil society; we document and denounce murders, disappearances, torture, arbitrary imprisonment, discrimination, and other abuses of internationally recognized human rights. Our goal is to hold governments accountable if they transgress the rights of their people.

Human Rights Watch began in 1978 with the founding of its Europe and Central Asia division (then known as Helsinki Watch). Today, it also includes divisions covering Africa, the Americas, Asia, and the Middle East. In addition, it includes three thematic divisions on arms, children's rights, and women's rights. It maintains offices in New York, Washington, Los Angeles, London, Brussels, Moscow, Dushanbe, Rio de Janeiro, and Hong Kong. Human Rights Watch is an independent, nongovernmental organization, supported by contributions from private individuals and foundations worldwide. It accepts no government funds, directly or indirectly.

The staff includes Kenneth Roth, executive director; Michele Alexander, development director; Reed Brody, advocacy director; Carroll Bogert, communications director;Cynthia Brown,program director; Barbara Guglielmo, finance director; Jeri Laber special advisor; Lotte Leicht, Brussels office director; Patrick Minges, publications director; Susan Osnos, associate director; Maria Pignataro Nielsen, human resources director; Jemera Rone, counsel; Wilder Tayler, general counsel; and Joanna Weschler, United Nations representative. Jonathan Fanton is the chair of the board. Robert L. Bernstein is the founding chair.

The regional directors of Human Rights Watch are Peter Takirambudde, Africa; José Miguel Vivanco, Americas; Sidney Jones, Asia; Holly Cartner, Europe and Central Asia; and Hanny Megally, Middle East and North Africa. The thematic division directors are Joost R. Hiltermann, arms; Lois Whitman, children's; and Regan Ralph, women's.

The members of the board of directors are Jonathan Fanton, chair; Lisa Anderson, Robert L. Bernstein, David M. Brown, William Carmichael, Dorothy Cullman, Gina Despres, Irene Diamond, Adrian W. DeWind, Fiona Druckenmiller, Edith Everett, Michael E. Gellert, Vartan Gregorian, Alice H. Henkin, James F. Hoge, Stephen L. Kass, Marina Pinto Kaufman, Bruce Klatsky, Joanne Leedom-Ackerman, Josh Mailman, Yolanda T. Moses, Samuel K. Murumba, Andrew Nathan, Jane Olson, Peter Osnos, Kathleen Peratis, Bruce Rabb, Sigrid Rausing, Orville Schell, Sid Sheinberg, Gary G. Sick, Malcolm Smith, Domna Stanton, John J. Studzinski, and Maya Wiley. Robert L. Bernstein is the founding chair of Human Rights Watch.

ACKNOWLEDGMENTS

This report was researched and written by Lee Tucker, consultant to the Children's Rights Division of Human Rights Watch. It was edited by Lois Whitman, Executive Director of the Children's Rights Division, and Michael McClintock, Deputy Program Director of Human Rights Watch. Other Human Rights Watch staff who assisted substantially in the review or preparation of this report were: Dinah PoKempner, Deputy General Counsel of Human Rights Watch; Jo Becker, Children's Rights Division Advocacy Director; Shalu Rozario, Children's Rights Division Associate; and Lance Compa, Program Researcher.

We are grateful to the many people and organizations who offered their assistance and expertise in connection with this report, not all of whom can be named. In particular, we thank: Diane Mull of the Association of Farmworker Opportunity Programs; Darlene Adkins of the National Consumers League Child Labor Coalition; Emma Torres, Coordinator of Bridges in Friendship: A Project of the Border Health Foundation; Gary Restaino, former staff attorney of Community Legal Services in Phoenix; Rupert Sandoval, Coordinator of the Arizona Interagency Farmworkers Coalition; David Dick and Maria Elena Badilla of Pinal-Gila Legal Aid Society; Janice Porter and Sister Emily Gezich of Aguila, Arizona; Blanca Rodriguez, United Farm Workers attorney in Sunnyside, Washington; Gina Lombardi of the National Center for Farmworker Health; Michelle Gonzalez Arroyo of the Labor Occupational Health Program at the University of California in Berkeley; and Dr. Marion Moses of the Pesticide Information Center. Dr. John Arnold of Project PPEP in Tucson offered great assistance by putting us in touch with several other Project PPEP staff members—teachers Karen Lowe, Jimmy Pruitt, and Doug Davidson, and regional directors Augie Zaragoza and Raoul Salazar—all of whom were extremely helpful and to whom we give our heartfelt thanks.

Many government officials gave graciously of their time, sharing information and responding to our queries. Our thanks to: Corlis Sellers, Libby Hendrix, and Esther LaPlante of the U.S. Department of Labor; Marcos Cordoba of the Arizona Department of Economic Security; Art Morelos of the Industrial Commission of Arizona; Frank Zamudio of the Arizona Department of Agriculture; Kevin Keaney of the Environmental Protection Agency; and Cindy O'Hara of the Equal Employment Opportunity Commission.

The Natural Resources Defense Council's excellent report, "Trouble on the Farm: Growing up with Pesticides in Agricultural Communities," was invaluable to our report and is cited numerous times. We gratefully acknowledge the NRDC and author Dr. Gina Solomon for this outstanding contribution, as well as their ongoing work aimed at protecting children from pesticides. We also acknowledge the National Research Council and the Institute of Medicine for their comprehensive 1998 book, *Protecting Youth at Work*, cited frequently in our report

Above all, Human Rights Watch would like to thank all of the children and youth who shared their experiences with us, making this report possible. In order to protect their privacy, all of their names have been changed except where otherwise noted.

TABLE OF CONTENTS

I. SUMMARY

Damaris A., now nineteen, started working in the broccoli and lettuce fields when she was thirteen years old and continued until she was nearly eighteen.[1] During the five months of peak season, she usually worked fourteen hours a day, with two fifteen-minute breaks and a half-hour for lunch. She often worked eighty-five or ninety hours a week. For months on end she suffered daily nosebleeds; several times her blood pressure plummeted and she nearly passed out. She was exposed to pesticide drift and fell ill, yet was required to keep working. "I just endured it," she said, of her time in the fields. "It was very difficult."

Mark H. was twelve the summer he first worked in the cotton fields of central Arizona, getting up at 3:00 a.m. and finishing work at 2:00 p.m. His parents, aunts, and uncles had all worked in the fields for years. "My dad started when he was ten years old, and he didn't finish 'til he was twenty-two," Mark H. said. Like his father, Mark H. missed a lot of school and eventually dropped out. Now nineteen years old, he is struggling to catch up on his education. "A lot of my friends worked the fields, and a lot dropped out. I was supposed to graduate last year and I didn't . . . I would tell kids just to finish school. You can't get a good job without a diploma. With a diploma you can go to college. You get more options."

Two years ago, when he was fifteen, Benjamin C. cut his finger badly with a broccoli-harvesting knife. "That knife was so sharp," he said, showing a three-inch long scar running the length of his finger. Instead of taking Benjamin C. to a local hospital or clinic, the field supervisor sent him home to his parents' house in Mexico; from there, his parents took him to a Mexican hospital. This delayed by two or three hours his medical care, and also circumvented the employer's responsibility under workers' compensation law. According to advocates, this is typical in the border region. "The foremen send them off with thirty bucks to Mexico," said one.

---

[1] This and all other children's names have been changed, except where otherwise noted.

1

In the fields, the United States is like a developing country[2]

Agricultural work is the most hazardous and grueling area of employment open to children in the United States.[3] It is also the least protected.

Hundreds of thousands of children and teens labor each year in fields, orchards, and packing sheds across the United States. They pick lettuce and cantaloupe, weed cotton fields, and bag produce. They climb rickety ladders into cherry orchards, stoop low over chili plants, and "pitch" heavy watermelons for hours on end. Many begin their work days—either in the fields or en route to the fields—in the middle of the night. Twelve-hour workdays are common.

These hardworking youth labor under more dangerous conditions than their contemporaries working in nonagricultural settings. They are routinely exposed to dangerous pesticides, sometimes working in fields still wet with poison, often given no opportunity to wash their hands before eating lunch. They risk heat exhaustion and dehydration, as their employers fail to provide enough water, or any at all. They suffer injuries from sharp knives, accidents with heavy equipment, falls from ladders. Repetitive motions in awkward and punishing poses can interfere with the proper growth of their bodies. Lack of sleep—because they are working too many hours—interferes with their schooling and increases their chances of injury. Depression affects them more often than other minors, a reflection of the cumulative stresses and burdens in their young lives. Only 55 percent of them will graduate from high school.

Farmworker youth face persistent wage exploitation and fraud. One-third of those interviewed by Human Rights Watch reported earnings that were significantly less than minimum wage. Some earned only two or three dollars an hour.

Incredibly, these juvenile workers are protected *less* under United States law than are juveniles working in safer occupations. Under the Fair Labor Standards Act (FLSA), children working on farms may be employed at a younger age than other working children—twelve (even younger under some circumstances) as opposed to fourteen. Employers may also work them for longer hours—in agriculture, there is no limit to the number of hours a child

---

[2] Darlene Adkins, Coordinator, Child Labor Coalition. Human Rights Watch telephone interview, January 25, 1999. The Child Labor Coalition, comprised of fifty member organizations, is part of the National Consumers League.

[3] Mining, the most dangerous occupation in the country, is not open to those under the age of eighteen. Agriculture is the second-most dangerous occupation overall.

may work. In all other occupations, children under the age of sixteen are limited to three hours of work a day when school is in session. Not only that, but the FLSA does not require overtime pay for agricultural work it does for other occupations. Finally, juveniles in agriculture may engage in hazardous work at the age of sixteen; for all other occupations, the minimum age for hazardous work is eighteen.

The Fair Labor Standards Act claims to prohibit "oppressive child labor." Yet the FLSA permits oppressive child labor in agriculture to continue. The FLSA's bias against farmworker children amounts to de facto race-based discrimination: an estimated 85 percent of migrant and seasonal farmworkers nationwide are racial minorities; in some regions, including Arizona, approximately 99 percent of farmworkers are Latino.[4] In addition to raising serious concerns under the Equal Protection clause of the U.S. Constitution, this discrimination may violate numerous provisions of international law.

It is discrimination in legal protection—de jure discrimination against farmworker children as opposed to other working children, with a doubly discriminatory effect against Latino children—that leads directly to deprivation of other rights, most notably the right to education and the right to health and safety. By allowing agricultural employers to work children for unlimited hours, United States law severely undermines their opportunity to participate fully in universal education. Longer hours worked also increase the risk to children of pesticide exposure, repetitive-motion disabilities, fatigue and injuries, and depression and substance abuse.

In addition, United States law and practice contravene various international law prohibitions on exploitative and harmful work by children, including standards set by the Convention on the Rights of the Child. The United States appears to be headed toward noncompliance with the 1999 ILO Worst Forms of Child Labor Convention as well, which will enter into force for the U.S. in December 2000. It requires that member governments prohibit and eliminate "the worst forms of child labor." The United States is off to a dubious start in this regard, having claimed that it is already in full compliance with the convention and that no change to law or practice is necessary.

The failings of the FLSA are not the only way that the United States leaves its young farmworkers unprotected. Congress exempts all farms with fewer than eleven employees from enforcement of Occupational Safety and Health Administration (OSHA) regulations. This affects many juvenile farmworkers' well-being directly, compromising their right to a clean and safe work environment.

---

[4] In the United States, "Latino" refers to people of Latin American ancestry.

The Environmental Protection Agency (EPA), meanwhile, offers no greater protection from pesticide contamination for child laborers than it does for adults. There is only one set of regulations and standards, which take as their model the adult male body. The fact that children's bodies are typically both smaller than adults' bodies and developmentally more vulnerable to pesticide-related damage has not been addressed. The results of this failure to protect children are potentially deadly and are emerging daily all across the United States.

Even to the limited extent that U.S. laws do protect farmworker youth, they are not adequately enforced. The Department of Labor, charged with enforcing the child labor, wage and hour provisions of the FLSA, cited only 104 cases of child labor violations in fiscal year 1998. (Estimates are that there are approximately one million violations related to child labor in U.S. agriculture each year.) The EPA leaves enforcement of its worker safety regulations to the individual states, but expresses little confidence in their ability to perform this task. The Occupational Safety and Health Administration, meanwhile, enforces its regulations in about half of the states, with the other half enforcing their own OSHA-approved "State Plans." Despite the fact that agriculture is second only to mining as the most hazardous occupation, a recent federal study found that OSHA devoted less than 3 percent of its inspections to agriculture. In Arizona, a State-Plan state, no farm inspections at all take place at the initiative of the Industrial Commission of Arizona, the enforcing agency.

The laws and enforcement practices of individual states are no better and sometimes worse. Many states don't even have minimum age requirements for children working in agriculture. All but a handful of states perform no enforcement whatsoever regarding juvenile labor in agriculture.

When violations are discovered and cited, growers frequently escape accountability by hiding behind the farm labor contractors they employ. Farm labor contractors act essentially as middlemen between the growers and the workers. They are paid by growers to hire the necessary workers, get them to the job site, ensure that the work is completed as desired, and pay the workers. When violations of the workers' rights are discovered, the growers frequently emerge untouched by fines and citations, on the grounds that the farm labor contractors and *only* the farm labor contractors are the workers' employers. For the most part, enforcement agencies have acquiesced to the growers on this point. Because farm labor contractors often have little money and no liability insurance, the result is that judgments and fines go unpaid and the workers remain uncompensated. Even when growers are cited and fined, however, sanctions are minimal and insufficient to deter future wrongdoing.

The result of these weak laws and enforcement efforts is that, as a practical matter, farmworking juveniles have second-class status: they enjoy fewer rights than their non-farmworking peers and they are exploited while the government looks the other way. They are vulnerable to occupational injury and illness because their jobs are dangerous; they are worked too hard because employers don't have to limit their hours; and they are underpaid because the growers and farm labor contractors can get away with it.

This report documents a wide range of troubling practices—some legal under current, inadequate domestic law, some blatantly illegal—that affect juvenile farmworkers. Most of these practices affect adult workers too. It is the widespread exploitation of adult workers, in fact, that contributes to the precarious situation of their sons and daughters who also must work in the fields.

If adult farmworkers were paid a living wage—as of 1999, average yearly earnings were less than $7,500—then their children would be under less pressure to begin working at such young ages and for such long hours. They would get more sleep and rest and more time to study. They would be less likely to drop out of school and, with a high school diploma, would have more options available to them.

This report recommends numerous changes to U.S. law. Key among them: that Congress amend the Fair Labor Standards Act to *protect all working children equally*. This means imposing, for the first time ever, limits on the number of hours children aged fifteen and younger can work in agriculture when school is in session.

Simultaneously with this, however, Congress and the administration must acknowledge that farmworker families need assistance on all fronts. Enforcement of workers' rights, assurance of adequate housing, increased availability of traditional and nontraditional education, free and accessible health care, and other assistance as necessary—these are the minimum conditions necessary to ensure that all children in the United States, including the children of agricultural laborers, have the possibility of a safe, dignified, and healthy start in life.

This report is based on interviews with more than thirty farmworker juveniles, most of them in Arizona, as well as with dozens of farmworker advocates and experts both in Arizona and nationally. The report also draws upon government officials in the areas of labor, agriculture, and health and safety. Except where otherwise noted, all names of farmworker children interviewed have been changed in this report for the protection of privacy and to guard against employer retaliation.

II. RECOMMENDATIONS

Human Rights Watch makes the following recommendations regarding the protection of juvenile farmworkers in the United States and urges their adoption as soon as possible:

To The United States Congress

- The Fair Labor Standards Act should be amended to increase the protection extended to juveniles working in agriculture. Such protection should conform with that offered to other working children in the United States and bring it into accord with international standards for the protection of children. Specifically, the act should be amended to:

    - Prohibit the employment of children aged thirteen and younger in agriculture, except for those working on farms owned and operated by their parents.
    - Limit the number of hours that children aged fourteen and fifteen can legally work in agriculture to: three hours a day on a school day and eighteen hours a week during a school week; eight hours a day on a nonschool day and forty hours a week when school is not in session.
    - Prohibit before-school agricultural work by children aged fifteen and younger. (Currently, there are no restrictions on early-morning agricultural work, although in nonagricultural occupations such work is forbidden for under-sixteen-year olds.)
    - Raise the minimum age for hazardous agricultural work to eighteen.

- In addition, The Fair Labor Standards Act should be amended to impose on sixteen and seventeen-year olds enrolled full time in school the same hourly restrictions on employment that apply to those fifteen and younger.

- Regarding application of the Occupational Safety and Health Act, Congress should halt its yearly approval of a rider exempting farms with ten or fewer employees from OSHA jurisdiction.

- Congress must address the educational and vocational needs of farmworkers. This is urgent, particularly for those juveniles who have already dropped out of school. The national program created for farmworker youth under the Workforce Investment Act of 1998 should be adequately funded to enable states to assist farmworker youth in completing their education and securing meaningful job training and placement assistance.

To the Wage and Hour Division, United States Department of Labor

- The Wage and Hour Division should dramatically increase agricultural workplace inspections targeting child labor and minimum wage violations. All violators should be sanctioned to the fullest extent of the law. Furthermore, serious, repeat, and willful violators should be actively publicized as such, both for deterrence purposes and to educate the public regarding child labor rights.

- The Wage and Hour Division should utilize The Fair Labor Standards Act's "hot goods" provision, which prohibits the interstate movement of goods produced in violation of child labor or minimum wage laws, whenever possible, favoring it over the traditional course of citations and relatively insignificant civil money penalties.

- Joint liability between farm labor contractors and growers should be pursued wherever possible in cases where a farm labor contractor has been found in violation of federal law.

- The Wage and Hour Division should initiate immediately a program of concerted collaboration with state child labor enforcement agencies and other child protection bodies. Such collaboration should encompass data-gathering and dissemination, the prioritization of enforcement goals, and strategies for achieving those goals according to available state and federal resources. At an absolute minimum, WHD should collect and review state enforcement data so as to determine the most urgent federal priorities and whether duplication of efforts is occurring.

- The Wage and Hour Division should collect, maintain, and disseminate statistics regarding the following:

  - The number of children working in agriculture, disaggregated by age and state and, to the extent possible, by race and ethnicity;
  - The number of children injured while working in agriculture each year, disaggregated by the type and severity of injury;

- The number of children sickened each year by occupational exposure to pesticides.

To The Occupational Safety and Health Administration (OSHA), United States Department of Labor, and to "State-Plan" States

- OSHA should vigorously enforce the Field Sanitation Regulations, which require employers to provide workers with drinking water, toilets, and handwashing facilities. Such enforcement must be proactive and include agency-initiated, unannounced inspections.

- OSHA should require that all states enforcing OSHA-approved "State Plans" do so in a vigorous manner, including frequent unannounced inspections.

- In all cases involving farm labor contractors, both federal OSHA and State-Plan states should initiate a policy of pursuing joint liability between farm labor contractors and growers.

- Both federal OSHA and State-Plan states should encourage other state and federal agencies to report all violations observed in the field; upon receipt of such information OSHA should immediately inspect the workplace in question.

- Both federal OSHA and State-Plan states should collect, maintain, and make available annual statistics regarding:

  - The number of inspections carried out at agricultural workplaces;
  - Whether those inspections were agency-initiated, were in response to information received from other agencies, or were the result of worker complaints; and
  - The results of the inspections, including abatements, citations, and fines.

- Both federal OSHA and State-Plan states should launch aggressive public education campaigns regarding field sanitation regulations; these campaigns should include toll-free numbers where workers and others can report complaints by telephone.

To The Environmental Protection Agency

- The Worker Protection Standard should be amended to:

    - Impose a minimum age of eighteen for all pesticide handlers;
    - Revise restricted-entry intervals (REIs), which prohibit entry into an area treated by pesticides for a specified period of time following the application of the chemicals. The revised REIs should distinguish between adults and children and impose more stringent REIs for children. The revised REIs also should incorporate an additional safety margin on top of what is determined necessary to ensure short and long-term safety, and should take into account the combined effect of both occupational and non-occupational exposures. The EPA currently uses an acute illness model that does not protect workers from long-term, chronic effects of pesticides.

- The EPA should closely monitor states' enforcement of the Worker Protection Standard and related pesticide regulations to ensure that such enforcement is vigorous and meaningful.

- The EPA should expand its program to educate workers regarding the Worker Protection Standard, and should ensure that materials used are culturally, age, and language appropriate.

- The EPA should ensure that state agencies responsible for enforcement of EPA regulations are staffed by a sufficient number of trained, bilingual (Spanish and English) compliance officers. Training should be offered to state compliance officers on an as-needed basis.

- The EPA should collect, maintain, and make available state enforcement statistics regarding farmworkers and pesticide safety.

To All States

- State child labor laws should be at least as protective as federal standards.

- All states should set or raise the minimum age for agricultural work to at least fourteen, with the exception of children working on farms owned and operated by their parents.

III. ADOLESCENT FARMWORKERS IN THE UNITED STATES: ENDANGERMENT AND EXPLOITATION

Introduction

Nobody knows how many adolescents work in agriculture in the United States. The General Accounting Office recently cited an estimate of 300,000 fifteen to seventeen-year olds working in agriculture each year, while acknowledging that "methodological problems . . . likely result in an undercounting of the total number."[5] This estimate excludes those fourteen and under; in fact, children under fourteen are not included in any nationally-based surveys of farmworkers. The United Farm Workers union estimates that there are 800,000 child farmworkers in the United States. These estimates include both children working as hired laborers and children working on their parents' farms—a much smaller group. This report focuses on children working as hired laborers.

Farmworkers aged seventeen and younger—all considered children under U.S. and international law[6]—can be found working all across the country. Particularly large populations of farmworkers live and work in California, Texas, Florida, Washington, and Arizona. Migrant streams travel up each year through the Midwest, the eastern seaboard, and into New York. Virtually no state is without child labor in agriculture, and certainly no state is without its fruits, as the produce that is harvested and packed by youngsters' hands may travel thousands of miles to grocery store shelves.

Farmworker interviews cited in this report took place primarily in Arizona, the United States' third-largest producer of vegetables and citrus. In addition to being a "base state"—a state with a significant resident farmworker population—Arizona is also one of several "source states," states from which migrant streams flow seasonally up and out into other parts of the country. Approximately 100,000 people work as farm laborers in Arizona.

Human Rights Watch interviewed both migrant and seasonal agricultural workers for this report. Migrant workers are those whose work requires them to be absent overnight from their permanent place of residence; in practice, many may be absent from their permanent homes for months at a time. Seasonal

---

[5] U.S. General Accounting Office, "Child Labor in Agriculture: Characteristics and Legality of Work," Washington, D.C.: U.S. General Accounting Office, 1998; GAO/HEHS-98-112R, p. 2.

[6] Article 1 of the Convention on the Rights of the Child states that "a child means every human being below the age of eighteen years unless under the law applicable to the child, majority is attained earlier."

agricultural workers are those whose work does not require an overnight absence from their permanent residences. The combined total of migrant and seasonal farmworkers in the United States is estimated at four million.[7]

Although our field research was concentrated in Arizona, the problems we encountered are national in scope and were corroborated by experts in various other states. Laws governing child labor in agriculture are inadequate and out of date, enforcement is lax, and sanctions against violators are insignificant. The differential treatment of children working in agriculture as opposed to children working in other occupations is indefensible and discriminatory.

Children come to agriculture at varying ages. Reports of children as young as four or five working alongside their parents are not uncommon.[8] Full time agricultural work, whether during school vacations and weekends or year-round, usually begins in early adolescence. The majority of workers interviewed for this report began working in the fields between the ages of thirteen and fifteen. A recent California study also reported thirteen to fifteen as the most common ages at which children begin agricultural work,[9] and a Florida study found most young farmworkers began working by the age of fourteen.[10]

Farm work is low-paid, exhausting, stigmatized, and often dangerous. Agricultural workers labor under extreme weather conditions, from pre-dawn cold to intense desert heat, where temperatures are commonly well above 100 degrees Fahrenheit. Their work is physically demanding, requiring sustained strength, endurance, and coordination.

Twelve-hour days are routine, as are six and seven-day work weeks. During peak harvesting seasons, children may work fourteen, sixteen, or even eighteen hours a day, seven days a week. Whether paid by the hour or on the

---

[7] The U.S. Department of Health and Human Services has estimated that there are 1.5 million migrant farmworkers and 2.5 million seasonal farmworkers. United States Department of Health and Human Services, Bureau of Primary Health Care homepage (http://www.bphc.hrsa.dhhs.gov/mhc/mhc1.htm; accessed August 24, 1999), p. 2.

[8] In Arizona, a July 1998 investigation by the U.S. Department of Labor turned up twelve underage children working in onion fields, including a four-year old. Graciela Sevilla, "Littlest Workers: Arizona Targeted in Child Labor Sweep," *Arizona Republic*, July 24, 1998. *Oregonian* in August 1998 reported finding dozens of farmworker children younger than twelve. Alex Pulaski, "Rules protecting children lost in fields of Northwest," *Oregonian*, August 30, 1998.

[9] Arroyo and Kurre, "Young Agricultural Workers in California," Labor Occupational Health Program, Center for Occupational and Environmental Health, School of Public Health, University of California, Berkeley, November 1997, pp. 18-20.

[10] Human Rights Watch telephone interview with Dr. Marion Moses, President, Pesticide Education Center, San Francisco, California, February 23, 1999.

basis of piece-rates, they are not paid overtime wages—the law does not require it.

Children undertake farm work because their families are extremely poor and no other work is available. Those who live near towns leap at the chance to work instead at a fast-food restaurant or supermarket. Those in rural areas often have literally no other employment opportunities available.

Farmworker Poverty

An intergenerational cycle of poverty plagues farmworkers. Most parents of farmworker children are themselves farmworkers. The average annual income for a *two-earner* farmworker family is just over $14,000 a year, [11] well below the official federal poverty level, which was $16,700 in 1999.[12] These low earnings make it difficult for farmworker parents to meet their family's needs, which in turn puts pressure on their children to earn money as soon as possible—usually in the fields. All of the juveniles interviewed by Human Rights Watch were children of farmworkers. All of them began working either in order to help their family meet their basic needs or in order to take care of their own needs—for example, buying clothes for school—because their parents were too poor to do so.

The earnings of both adult and child farm laborers are low for several reasons. To begin with, agricultural work pays poorly: hourly rates are rarely higher than minimum wage—$5.15 as of June 2000—while piece-rate wages under the best of conditions rarely result in an hourly wage above $7.00—and often result in an hourly wage significantly below minimum wage, especially for children. Overtime wages are not paid, as federal law exempts agriculture from this requirement.   Furthermore, because the work is seasonal and workers usually must move to follow the crops, weeks and even months may go by during which no income at all is brought in.

According to farmworker advocates and workers themselves, unscrupulous employers further cut away at earnings with the following common practices:

- Not paying the workers for their last two weeks of work at the end of the season;

---

[11] National Center for Farmworker Health, "Who are America's Farmworkers?" (http://www.ncfh.org/aboutfws/aboutfws.htm, accessed March 22, 1999), p. 2.   In Arizona, average farmworker earnings are $6,200 a year.   Human Rights Watch telephone interview with Janine Duron, Department of Economic Security, Yuma, Arizona, September 18, 1998.

[12] *Federal Register*, vol. 64, no. 52, March 18, 1999, pp. 13428-13430.

- Withholding social security payments, but then pocketing the money instead of reporting it to the federal government;

- Deducting from workers' pay the cost of work-related equipment provided by the employer, including safety equipment that the government requires employers to provide;

- Deducting from workers' pay the supposed costs of providing worker housing (which fewer and fewer employers do). One Arizona employer, for example, reportedly deducted from his workers' pay the entire cost of his ranch's use of electricity, despite the fact that the workers lived in shacks lighted with a single bulb each;

- Deducting from workers' pay a fee for transporting them to and from the work site. For some workers, transportation time and expenses represent a huge burden. Workers transported from the Yuma area of Arizona to the agricultural area west of Phoenix, for example, travel two and a half hours each way, for which they reportedly pay $12 of their $40 daily wage.

- Failing to provide drinking water as required by law, and then selling workers soda or beer for $1 or $1.50 each.

Vulnerability of Farmworkers

Children, being inexperienced and often unassertive, are even more vulnerable to wage exploitation than are adults. It is important to note, though, that all farmworkers, especially those not unionized or otherwise organized,[13] are very vulnerable to exploitation and abuse. Despite the recurring push by growers and some politicians for a "guestworker" program to bring in more farmworkers from other countries—primarily Mexico—from the workers' perspective there is already an abundance of labor competing for the same grueling jobs. "There is lots of mistreatment at work by the farm labor contractors, by the foremen. They know if they kick one person out, there will be ten more waiting to take the job," explains Emma Torres, coordinator of a

---

[13] Agricultural workers are explicitly excluded from coverage under the National Labor Relations Act, and therefore have no federally-guaranteed right of unionization and collective bargaining.

border health initiative and a member of the National Advisory Council on Migrant Health. "So the workers don't complain. Anything is better than no job."[14]

The dismal state of the Mexican economy is another factor in the competition for agricultural jobs in the United States. As of early 2000, the daily minimum wage in Mexico was equivalent to approximately four U.S. dollars.[15]

Workers are further vulnerable because of language barriers, as many do not speak English, unfamiliarity with U.S. worker protection laws and how to obtain assistance, and geographical isolation. Many farmworkers work and live in areas that are hours from the nearest city and far removed even from towns. "It's a whole different world," said Amelia Lopez, a former outreach worker in western Arizona. "There is no one there. There is no housing. They [the workers] don't have anyone to back them up. . . . I encountered a lot of people with blisters on their hands and with health issues from pesticides. When they confronted their employer they were fired—gone the next day."[16]

In areas where a single grower is the only employer, control over workers can be intense, even in their nonworking hours. Several advocates and government employees told Human Rights Watch that they had been denied access to certain growers' lands, and that workers were too intimidated to speak to them even when off the property of the grower.

Investigator Frank Zamudio of the Arizona Department of Agriculture's Pesticide Worker Safety program was denied access to Pavich Farms, a prominent organic grape grower; he had to threaten to get a search warrant before he was finally allowed onto the land. "The situation there is hostile, suspicious," he said. "Workers won't talk [to government workers] on the premises."[17]

Human Rights Watch witnessed employer intimidation of workers during a visit to the town of Aguila, Arizona, which is surrounded by the cantaloupe fields of Martori Farms/Eagle Produce, Inc., operating on land leased from the state of Arizona. Martori is virtually the only employer in Aguila—"you either

---

[14] Human Rights Watch interview with Emma Torres, Project Coordinator, Bridges in Friendship (a project of the Border Health Foundation), Somerton, Arizona, September 30, 1998.

[15] See , accessed May 14, 2000.

[16] Human Rights Watch telephone interview with Amelia Lopez, former Arizona Department of Economic Security outreach worker, March 18, 1999.

[17] Human Rights Watch interview with Frank Zamudio, Arizona Department of Agriculture Pesticide Worker Safety Investigator, Yuma, Arizona, October 1, 1998.

work with them [Martori] or you don't work," according to former outreach worker Amelia Lopez. Two adolescent girls took Human Rights Watch to see the company-owned single barracks room where their family of six had previously lived—a tiny hot room with a battered old school locker, a stained mattress, and thousands of flies swarming outside. Upon our return to the girls' house, we learned that a Martori Farms employee had come by the house to warn the girls' parents—both of whom work for Martori—that the company "could take the girls to court" for their association with us.

Farm Labor Contractors

Farm labor contractors are central to the structure of agricultural production in the United States. Farm labor contractors range in size from single individuals to large corporations. Under contract to a grower, a farm labor contractor typically is responsible for hiring and overseeing the workers and ensuring that the work—planting, pruning, weeding, harvesting, etc.—is completed satisfactorily. Farm labor contractors usually are paid a lump sum by the growers, which they then use to secure labor as needed.

Government agencies and some courts often operate on the assumption that *only* the farm labor contractor, and not the grower, is the employer of the farmworker. Either the employer or the farm labor contractor might set the rate at which wages will be paid, but it is the farm labor contractor who recruits and contracts with the workers, pays the wages, is responsible for payroll deductions, and often transports the workers to the work site each day (usually for a fee). Where a farm labor contractor is used, the grower may have no direct contact with the workers.

This arrangement is problematic in that it allows growers to evade responsibility in the event of wage disputes, health and safety violations, or other unfair or illegal practices. Often, a grower who utilized a farm labor contractor can avoid responsibility for illegal acts and omissions on the grounds that the farm labor contractor, and not the grower, was the "employer." Farm labor contractors generally have fewer resources than growers and are less likely to satisfy judgments or fines that have been levied against them. They are more likely to be un- or underinsured. Farm labor contractors can also be very flexible. Although prohibited by law, it is not unusual for farm labor contractors to evade responsibility for violations by closing down operations, only to later resume under a different name, for example by using a relative as a fraudulent front-person in the Department of Labor certification process.

Health and Safety Risks

Children working in agriculture face an alarming array of dangers. On a daily basis they may be exposed to carcinogenic pesticides, dramatically unsanitary conditions, heat-related illnesses, and hazardous equipment. Their immature and still-growing bodies are more vulnerable than adults' bodies to systemic damage, and their lack of experience makes them more susceptible to accidents and work-related sicknesses.

Despite their greater vulnerability, children are afforded no more protection than adults—to the contrary, they essentially receive *less* protection, in that health and safety standards now in place have been formulated with adults in mind. The Environmental Protection Agency's (EPA) pesticide reentry intervals (REIs) for example—which set the minimum period of time that workers must be kept out of a field after pesticides have been applied—are determined using the model of a 154-pound male.[18] Nor do Occupational Safety and Health Administration standards take into account the special risks facing children.[19]

Pesticides

When I was fourteen I worked in the fields for two weeks, chopping the weeds around the cotton plants. . . . I woke up one night, I couldn't breathe; I was allergic to something they were spraying in the fields. I stopped breathing . . . I tried to drink water but I couldn't so I ran into my mom's room 'cause I didn't have no air in me and I was like [wheezing gasps] trying to get air in there but I couldn't . . .
At the hospital they said I was allergic to something out there . . . something they were spraying. . . . They sprayed the fields in the morning. We'd be out there when they were doing it, or when they were leaving, or we could see them doing other fields. They'd spray by plane.   —Richard M., seventeen years old[20]

---

[18] United States General Accounting Office, "Pesticides: Improvements Needed to Ensure the Safety of Farmworkers and their Children," Washington, D.C.: U.S. General Accounting Office, March 2000, GAO/RCED-00-40, p. 19.

[19] See National Research Council and Institute of Medicine, *Protecting Youth at Work: Health, Safety, and Development of Working Children and Adolescents in the United States* (Washington, D.C.: National Academy Press, 1998), pp. 173-174. Furthermore, almost all OSHA standards do not apply to agricultural workplaces. Ibid., p. 174.

[20] Human Rights Watch interview, Casa Grande, Arizona, October 27, 1998. Wheezing is a symptom of pesticide poisoning. Natural Resources Defense Council, *Trouble on the Farm*, p. 5.

On June 27, 1997, seventeen-year-old migrant farmworker José Antonio Casillas collapsed and died while riding his bike near his home in rural Utah. Emergency workers found white foam streaming from his nose. According to José's uncle, the day before he died the boy had been soaked with pesticide sprayed from a tractor; a week earlier he had also been sprayed, while working in a peach orchard. After the second spraying he showed symptoms of severe pesticide poisoning, including vomiting, sweating, diarrhea and headaches. He had received no training from his employer regarding pesticide dangers and the symptoms of exposure, and reportedly slept in his pesticide-soaked clothing the night before his death.[21]

Exposure to pesticides is a serious risk to all farmworkers. The Environmental Protection Agency estimates that as many as 300,000 farmworkers suffer pesticide poisoning each year,[22] while the Natural Resources Defense Council estimates as many as 40,000 *physician-diagnosed* poisonings occur each year.[23] Only a small percentage of pesticide-related illnesses are reported to government or health officials.[24]

Few studies have been undertaken regarding pesticide exposure levels among agricultural workers—and none regarding juvenile farmworkers—but those that have show high rates of contamination. Workers in Washington apple

---

[21] Association of Farmworker Opportunity Programs, "Did Pesticides Kill José Antonio Casillas?" *Washington Newsline*, http://www.afop.org/newsletter/july98/pesticide.html.

[22] United States General Accounting Office, "Hired Farmworkers: Health and Well-Being at Risk," Washington, D.C.: U.S. General Accounting Office, 1992; GAO/HRD-092-46, p. 3.

[23] Natural Resources Defense Council, *Trouble on the Farm: Growing Up with Pesticides in Agricultural Communities* (New York: Natural Resources Defense Council, October 1998), p. 6.

[24] According to a draft report by the Arizona Department of Environmental Quality, both the federal General Accounting Office and the Arizona Department of Health and Safety found, in separate studies, "a serious problem" of underreporting of pesticide-related illnesses. Arizona Department of Environmental Quality, "Occupational Exposure to Toxic Materials and Pesticides," p. 2, http://earthvision.asu.edu/acerp/section3/Chp_12HH.html. The primary author of this report was Tim Flood, M.D., Medical Director, Chronic Disease Epidemiology, Arizona Department of Health.

orchards, for example, were found to have sixteen times more pesticide residue in their urine than their nonfarmworker neighbors.[25]

Thousands of pesticides are registered with the EPA and currently in use in U.S. fields.[26] Three hundred and fifty are registered for use on food crops.[27] At least 101 are probable or possible human carcinogens.[28] In addition to cancer, pesticide exposure has been linked repeatedly to brain damage, endocrine (hormone) disruption, and birth defects.[29]

The risks are particularly acute for children. In 1998, the Natural Resources Defense Council (NRDC) released *Trouble on the Farm: Growing Up with Pesticides in Agricultural Communities,* a comprehensive report detailing the dangers to children of pesticide exposure. According to the NRDC:

> Children and infants are uniquely at risk from pesticides both because of physiological susceptibility and greater relative exposure. . . .[30]

> [T]heir bodies cannot efficiently detoxify and eliminate chemicals, their organs are still growing and developing, and . . . they have a longer lifetime to develop health complications after an exposure. [Furthermore], children are disproportionately exposed to pesticides compared with adults due to their greater intake of food, water, and air per unit of body weight.[31]

---

[25] Matt Crenson, "Pesticides May Jeopardize Child Farmworkers' Health," *Children for Hire*, an Associated Press series, December 9, 1997.

[26] Youth Advocate Program International, "U.S. Farmworker Children Lack Needed Workplace Protection," *Youth Advocate Program International Report*, vol. 3, no. 1, Spring 1998, http://www.yapi.org/rpt.htm, p. 3.

[27] Learning Disabilities Association of America et al., "Request that Pesticides be Tested for their Toxicity to the Developing Nervous System," letter to Carol Browner of the Environmental Protection Agency, May 12, 1999, p. 2. The letter was signed also by Consumers Union, Natural Resources Defense Council, Science and Environmental Health Network, Physicians for Social Responsibility, and the U.S. Public Interest Research Group.

[28] Natural Resources Defense Council, *Trouble on the Farm*, p. 8, citing Dr. Lynn Goldman of the U.S. Environmental Protection Agency.

[29] See Ibid., pp. 7-9.

[30] Natural Resources Defense Council, *Trouble on the Farm*, p. 12.

[31] Ibid., p. viii.

Children and adults working in the fields may be exposed to pesticides in a variety of ways, including: working in a field where pesticides have recently been applied; breathing in pesticide "drift" from adjoining or nearby fields; working in a pesticide-treated field without appropriate protective gear, such as gloves and masks; eating with pesticide-contaminated hands; eating contaminated fruits and vegetables; and eating in a pesticide-contaminated field. Fields are typically sprayed with pesticides on a weekly basis.[32]

Workers may also be exposed to pesticides if they drink from, wash their hands, or bathe in irrigation canals or holding ponds, where pesticides can accumulate. Despite the fact that such practices are commonly reported and known to occur frequently, the pesticide level of irrigation canals and holding ponds is not monitored.[33]

Immediate signs of acute pesticide poisoning include nausea, vomiting, diarrhea, wheezing, rashes, headaches, and dizziness.[34] Long-term consequences may include childhood leukemia, kidney tumors, brain tumors, brain damage, and learning and memory problems.[35]

Many of the children interviewed by Human Rights Watch reported being exposed to pesticides and experiencing one or more symptoms of pesticide exposure, most commonly headaches, nausea and vomiting, rashes, and dizziness. Some were subjected to pesticide drift when adjacent fields were sprayed while they were working. Others noticed the smell of pesticides in the fields where they worked and saw residue on leaves.

When they sprayed—usually once a week—we would leave the field for half an hour.

---

[32] Human Rights Watch interview with Frank Zamudio, Arizona Department of Agriculture Pesticide Worker Safety Investigator, Yuma, Arizona, October 1, 1998.

[33] Arizona Department of Environmental Quality, "Occupational Exposure to Toxic Materials and Pesticides," p. 11, http://earthvision.asu.edu/acerp/section3/Chp_12HH.html.

[34] Natural Resources Defense Council, *Trouble on the Farm*, pp. 6, 23.

[35] Natural Resources Defense Council, "Farm Children Face Hazards from Agricultural Chemicals," press release, October 22, 1998, p. 1.

Once they sprayed the field right next to where we were working. We all got horrible headaches. One woman was vomiting. The foreman sent her home, but the rest of us had to keep working.

—Damaris A., nineteen years old[36]

We would smell pesticides once in awhile in the fields. We would get headaches and rashes. Red and itchy rashes all over our hands and wrists. For two or three days the rash would stay. We would tell our supervisors, and they would say "it's normal—it's from the plants." We know it's not from the plants! But we'd have to keep working anyway.

—Dina V., nineteen years old[37]

None of the youth interviewed for this report had received training regarding the dangers of pesticides, safe usage, preventive measures, or what to do in the event of exposure. Such training is required by the Worker Protection Standard of the EPA.[38]

Some of the teens interviewed did not even know what pesticides were. Javier P., who began working in cotton and onion fields at the age of fourteen, responded to a question about pesticides by saying, "Pesticides? Was that the medicine they put on [the crops]? No, I don't know anything about that."[39]

Others were unaware of the dangers and symptoms of pesticide poisoning. A fifteen-year old girl, for example, reported that many of her friends had become sick and thrown up while picking strawberries. She attributed these

---

[36] Human Rights Watch interview, Somerton, Arizona, October 1, 1998. Damaris A. had been a field worker since the age of thirteen, primarily in the Yuma area and in western Arizona.

[37] Human Rights Watch interview, Aguila, Arizona, April 29, 1999.

[38] Code of Federal Regulations, Title 40, Part 170. Agricultural workers must be trained by their employer—unless they show proof of previous training within five years—regarding the hazards of pesticides, where and in what form pesticides may be encountered, routes through which pesticides can enter the body, signs and symptoms of pesticide poisoning, emergency first aid for pesticide poisoning and how to obtain emergency medical care, decontamination techniques, hazards from drift, hazards from pesticide residues on clothing, and an explanation of other protective Worker Protection Standard requirements, including application and entry restrictions and the required posting of warning signs. United States Environmental Protection Agency, *The Worker Protection Standard for Agricultural Pesticides—How to Comply* (U.S. Government Printing Office: Washington, 1993).

[39] Human Rights Watch interview, Willcox, Arizona, March 16, 1999.

illnesses, however, to "lots of germs on the fruit," and said her friends "got the flu from working in strawberries."[40]

Human Rights Watch spoke with a boy who, when he was sixteen years old, spent a summer using a pesticide backpack sprayer to treat weeds growing in the corn fields of a local landowner. Twice a day, three times a week, he mixed the pesticide and then sprayed it to cover the weeds' leaves. Asked if he wore gloves, a mask, or any protective clothing, he waved his hand dismissively and said "Naw . . ." The landowner had told him it was nothing to worry about.[41]

The Fair Labor Standards Act enumerates "Exposure to agricultural chemicals classified as Category I or II of toxicity" as hazardous agricultural conditions. Accordingly, on a farm where the FLSA applies, children aged fifteen and under are prohibited from handling category I and category II pesticides. They may still handle pesticides of lower toxicity, while juveniles aged sixteen and older work without any pesticide-related restrictions.

The EPA's Worker Protection Standard regulates workers' involvement with pesticides. It requires, among other things, the training of all workers involved in mixing or applying pesticides, and the use of protective equipment and clothing when handling pesticides. It does not set any minimum age requirement for mixing or applying pesticides. A separate EPA regulation sets restricted-entry intervals. REIs are no more stringent for juveniles than for adults, despite the heightened risk of juveniles to suffer pesticide-related illnesses or injuries.

Although there have been very few studies to date regarding pesticide exposure among children and youth working in agriculture, the data that do exist suggest that such exposure is commonplace. A 1990 study of migrant farmworker children in New York State found that more than 40 percent had worked in fields still wet with pesticides, and 40 percent had been sprayed with pesticides, either directly from crop duster airplanes or indirectly from drift.[42]

Juvenile farmworkers, as is the case with all farmworkers, have very little power to protect themselves from the danger of pesticides or other health risks

---

[40] Human Rights Watch interview with Tiffany B., age fifteen, Casa Grande, Arizona, November 3, 1998.

[41] Human Rights Watch interview with Thomas K., Willcox, Arizona, March 16, 1999.

[42] Natural Resources Defense Council, *Trouble on the Farm*, p. 18 (citing Pollack, S. et al, "Pesticide exposure and working conditions among migrant farmworker children in western New York State," American Public Health Association Annual Meeting, 1990.)

in the fields. If they complain they are likely to be, at best, ignored. At worst, they will be fired. "I encountered a lot of people with blisters and [pesticide-related] health issues," an outreach worker told Human Rights Watch. "When they confronted their farm labor contractor or employer they were fired—gone the next day."[43]

Children's cumulative exposure to pesticides from all sources, including food, water, dust, and air, is already a source of concern for health professionals.[44] Additional exposure in the fields makes the risk more urgent still.

Children who live on or near agricultural land, or whose families work in the fields . . . are likely to be the most pesticide-exposed subgroup in the United States... . . . Many of the children with the greatest pesticide exposures are from migrant farmworker families . . . [F]arm children face particularly significant health risks.[45]

Under pressure from a variety of medical, scientific, farmworker, and children's advocacy organizations, the EPA is evaluating current protections for children and assessing their adequacy. "We're concerned that children may be a special population in need," an EPA official acknowledged to Human Rights Watch.[46] To date, though, the EPA has not taken concrete steps to increase the protection of juveniles working in agriculture or other children living on or near farms.

Sanitation

Drinking water, water for hand washing, and toilet facilities are the minimum sanitation requirements imposed by OSHA on farms. Even these minimal requirements, however, are often ignored by growers and by the farm labor contractors who bring in workers. Furthermore, Congress prohibits enforcement of these regulations on farms with ten employees or less, essentially exempting small farms from having to protect their workers' most

---

[43] Human Rights Watch telephone interview with Amelia Lopez, former Arizona Department of Economic Security outreach worker in western Arizona, March 18, 1999.

[44] See generally Natural Resources Defense Council, *Trouble on the Farm*, chapter five ("Surrounded by Pesticides").

[45] Natural Resources Defense Council, *Trouble on the Farm*, p. vii.

[46] Human Rights Watch telephone interview with Kevin Keaney, EPA Branch Chief for Certification and Worker Protection, October 19, 1999.

basic health and dignity requirements.[47] An estimated 95 percent of all United States farms fall under this exemption.[48]

State occupational safety and health requirements may be more or less stringent than federal, or more stringent in some respects but less protective in others.   In Arizona, for example, state occupational safety and health requirements apply to all farms with five or more employees, thereby covering many more workers than does federal OSHA.[49] On the other hand, Arizona state regulations only require one toilet for every forty workers, as opposed to the federal OSHA requirement of one toilet per twenty workers.[50]

Nearly all of the children interviewed by Human Rights Watch for this report said that they had worked in fields or orchards where one or more of these three basic requirements—drinking water, hand-washing facilities, and toilet facilities—was not met. Similar findings were reported in California and North Carolina surveys by others.[51]

Lack of Toilet Facilities
In Arizona, comments regarding toilet facilities included:

Portapotties? [Laughs.] No. Every place I've ever been, you just take tissue paper and find a hole.

—John P., age eighteen[52]

---

[47] Congress exempts small farms from enforcement of all OSHA standards by attaching riders to annual appropriations bills. See National Research Council and Institute of Medicine, *Protecting Youth at Work*, p. 174.

[48] National Research Council and Institute of Medicine, *Protecting Youth at Work*, p. 159.

[49] Human Rights Watch interview with Art Morelos, Compliance Supervisor for the Industrial Commission of Arizona, Division of Occupational Safety and Health, Tucson, Arizona, October 15, 1998.

[50] Industrial Commission of Arizona, Division of Occupational Safety and Health, Field Sanitation Regulation R4-13-670; U.S. Department of Labor, Occupational Safety and Health Administration, Fact Sheet No. OSHA 92-25, "OSHA's Field Sanitation Standard."

[51] In North Carolina, a survey found that only 4 percent of farmworkers had access to drinking water, handwashing facilities, and toilets. National Center for Farmworker Health,   "Who   Are   America's   Farmworkers?," http://www.ncfh.org/aboutfws/aboutfws.htm, p. 5. In California, a survey of several hundred adolescents working in agriculture found that they "repeatedly mentioned" lack of clean bathrooms and accessible drinking water as key concerns. Arroyo and Kurre, "Young Agricultural Workers in California," p. 37.

[52] Human Rights Watch interview, Willcox, Arizona, March 16, 1999.

No, I never saw a portapotty.[53] *I wouldn't expect a portapotty.*
                                                    —Ricky N., age seventeen[54]

They [portapotties] are too nasty to use. Sometimes they're near,
sometimes they're far, but it doesn't matter because no one will use
them anyway. Even at the beginning of the season they're horrible.
You either have to find another spot or hold it. I usually try to hold it.
                                                    —Sylvia R., age eighteen[55]

A top official of the Occupational Safety and Health Division of the
Industrial Commission of Arizona—often referred to as "state OSHA" or
"Arizona OSHA"—told Human Rights Watch that a lack of toilets was, together
with a lack of drinking cups, the "biggest complaint in the fields."[56]
Notwithstanding this, the same official also reported that his agency, which is
responsible for enforcing state sanitation regulations, does not do farm
inspections on its own initiative and does not do surprise inspections.[57] He was
unable to provide Human Rights Watch with statistics regarding citations for
sanitation-related violations in agriculture.

Lack of usable toilet facilities is unsanitary and contributes to the spread of
parasitic infection among workers. It can also be particularly dangerous and
humiliating for girls and women, in that it leaves them with the unpleasant
choice of either public urination—more obvious and awkward for females—or
urinary retention. Urinary retention is a cause of urinary tract infections, which
are suffered by farmworkers at a higher rate than the general population.[58] A
desire to avoid urination may also lead workers to limit their fluid intake, with
potentially grave, even deadly, consequences.

---

[53] A "portapotty" is a portable toilet.

[54] Human Rights Watch interview, Casa Grande, Arizona, October 27, 1998.

[55] Human Rights Watch interview, Aguila, Arizona, April 29, 1999.

[56] Human Rights Watch interview with Art Morelos, Compliance Supervisor,
Industrial Commission of Arizona, Division of Occupational Safety and Health, October
15, 1998, Tucson, Arizona.

[57] Ibid.

[58] National Center for Farmworker Health, "Who Are America's Farmworkers?" pp.
5-6.

Lack of Handwashing Facilities

Both federal and state occupational safety and health laws require agricultural employers to provide their workers with soap and water for handwashing. Only about half of the teens interviewed for this report said that handwashing facilities were available at their work sites.

Being unable to wash their hands with soap and water increases farmworkers' risk of pesticide poisoning. Pesticide residue on the plants transfers to workers' hands and arms, where it remains until they are able to wash it off. If this is not possible while at work, their skin can remain contaminated for twelve hours or more—however long it takes them to get home and wash—greatly prolonging their pesticide exposure.

Unwashed hands also virtually guarantee that pesticides will be ingested when workers eat their lunch. Workers typically break for thirty minutes for lunch, often sitting right in the fields to eat or moving to the edges of the fields when shade is available.

> There was no water for washing hands. Women on the packing
> tractor can wear gloves but when we picked we just used our hands.
> Then we would eat our lunch. There was no way to wash our hands
> first.
>
> —Sylvia R., eighteen, discussing her work picking
> cantaloupes the previous summer[59]

When employers don't provide handwashing facilities, workers may resort to washing in irrigation ditches, which are unclean and often contaminated with fertilizer and pesticide runoff.[60] Or the employers or field supervisors may themselves provide dirty and contaminated water to the workers. "Occasionally farm labor contractors will get water from the ditches or drainage canals and put it in a container as water for the employees to wash their hands with," reported a compliance supervisor with Arizona's Occupational Safety and Health

---

[59] Human Rights Watch interview, Aguila, Arizona, April 29, 1999.

[60] See Ibid., p. 4. Farmworkers' use of irrigation canals to bathe and wash was reported to Human Rights Watch by several farmworkers and farmworker advocates, including Augie Zaragoza, Director of Project PPEP's Casa Grande office (Human Rights Watch interview August 10, 1998, Casa Grande, Arizona), David Dick and Maria Elena Badilla, Director and Paralegal respectively of Pinal-Gila Legal Aid in Coolidge, Arizona (Human Rights Watch telephone interview, September 1, 1998), and Amelia Lopez, former Arizona Department of Economic Security outreach worker (Human Rights Watch telephone interview, March 18, 1999).

Division.[61] Such water exposes workers to dangerous chemicals and to organic wastes and parasites.

Lack of Drinking Water

Physical labor under hot conditions can rapidly overwhelm the body. Without adequate fluid intake and rest, workers risk devastating dehydration and heat-induced illness, up to and including death. (Heat illness is discussed in the following section.)

The U.S. Occupational Safety and Health Administration and the Environmental Protection Agency recommend that workers laboring under hot weather conditions drink a minimum of eight ounces of water every half-hour.[62] Very high heat or humidity increases the amount of recommended water, so that, for example, a person working in 90 degree heat under a full sun should drink eight ounces of water every fifteen minutes.[63]

Federal and state occupational safety and health laws require agricultural employers to supply sufficient amounts of cool water to their workers. [64] OSHA estimates "Sufficient" at "two to three gallons per worker on a hot day."[65] Arizona *requires* a minimum of two gallons per employee per day of "suitably cool" water.[66] Only some growers and farm labor contractors comply with this requirement. Many provide inadequate amounts of water, water that is hot or warm, or no drinking water at all.

Still others provide contaminated water. An Arizona farm was cited in 1997, for example, for providing farmworkers with water contaminated by E. coli, dangerous and potentially fatal bacteria.[67] An owner of the business, Texas

---

[61] Human Rights Watch interview with Art Morelos, Compliance Supervisor, Industrial Commission of Arizona, Division of Occupational Safety and Health, October 15, 1998, Tucson, Arizona.

[62] United States Environmental Protection Agency, "A Guide to Heat Stress in Agriculture," EPA-750-b-92-001, May 1993, pp. 17-19.

[63] Ibid.

[64] See, for example, 29 C.F.R. 1928.110 (the federal Occupational Safety and Health Administration's Field Sanitation Standard) and Arizona Industrial Commission Regulation R4-13-670 (Field Sanitation).

[65] Ibid., p. 24.

[66] Arizona Industrial Commission Regulation R4-13-670.

[67] Industrial Commission of Arizona, Division of Occupational Safety and Health, Inspection Report, Case Number 126996610, September 19, 1997 (reviewed by Human Rights Watch).

Hill Farms, confirmed to state inspectors that canal water was being given to the farm laborers; office workers were provided with different, uncontaminated water.[68] The same farm was also cited for failing to provide toilet and handwashing facilities to its agricultural workers. The Arizona Industrial Commission Division of Occupational Safety and Health assessed a total penalty against the business of $2,250 ($1,250 for providing contaminated water and $1,000 for the lack of toilet facilities).

Many teens reported that their foremen or farm labor contractors would bring one five or ten-gallon jug to the work site; when it was gone, no more water was brought in.

> We had to share water from one big jug. It wasn't enough. You couldn't drink as much as you wanted. Maybe twice a week we would run out of water completely.
>
> An old man took us there [to the field] in the morning, set us up, then would come back in the afternoon to pick us up. If you ran out of water, if you passed out, tough.
>
> —Ricky N., age seventeen[69]

Other young workers told Human Rights Watch that they had to bring their own drinking water.[70] Still others bought beverages from co-workers or supervisors who, in lieu of providing water, sold sodas or beer for $1.00 to $1.50 each.

> The supervisors sold beer for one dollar each. Lots of supervisors did this. People buy it because they are thirsty, not because they want to drink alcohol. They [supervisors] also sell it to teenagers—whoever. They don't care about your age. . . . People might buy several beers in a shift.
>
> —Sylvia R., age eighteen[71]

---

[68] Ibid

[69] Human Rights Watch interview, Casa Grande, Arizona, October 27, 1998.

[70] A California survey found that 75 percent of adolescent farmworkers brought their own water to work. Arroyo and Kurre, "Young Agricultural Workers in California," p. 31.

[71] Human Rights Watch interview, Aguila, Arizona, April 29, 1999.

[Some] farm labor contractors take out an ice chest filled with Coke, charge a dollar or a dollar-fifty for a Coke—this is economic exploitation. [Selling beer] is a health and safety issue.
—Art Morelos, Compliance Supervisor, Arizona OSHA[72]

Federal OSHA discourages consumption of soda by agricultural workers (the gases make it difficult to drink sufficiently large quantities of fluids) and warns strongly against the consumption of alcohol:

Alcohol affects the body's temperature-regulating capacities and increases the risk of heat-induced illness. . . . Workers should be strongly urged not to drink any alcohol during hot weather before starting work and until the end of the evening meal after work in order to give their body a chance for full replacement of all lost fluid.[73]

In addition to the risk of dehydration and heat illness, on-the-job consumption of alcohol increases the risk of injury from heavy equipment, knives, hoes, ladders, and other farming implements. A paralegal told Human Rights Watch that a seventeen-year old boy was killed in early summer 1998 in the cantaloupe fields near Aguila, a remote town northwest of Phoenix. He and other workers on the crew reportedly were drinking beer as they worked. Drunk, the boy slipped in front of the melon conveyor tractor and was killed.[74]

Hazardous Conditions; Work-Related Illnesses

Heat Illnesses

Heat illnesses can lead to death or brain-damage and are an ever-present danger for field workers. The EPA and OSHA estimate approximately 500

---

[72] Human Rights Watch interview, Tucson, Arizona, October 15, 1998.

[73] United States Environmental Protection Agency, "A Guide to Heat Stress in Agriculture," EPA-750-b-92-001, May 1993, pp.24-25.

[74] Human Rights Watch telephone interview with Maria Elena Badilla, paralegal with Pinal-Gila Legal Aid, Coolidge, Arizona, September 1, 1998. According to Badilla, the boy's body was returned to Mexico and no worker's compensation or other claim was filed.

deaths annually from heat illnesses in the United States.[75]   Children are more susceptible to heat stress than adults.[76]

The following coroner's report of a farmworker's death illustrates the deadliness of heat illness and the difficulty in treating a worker once the illness has progressed to a critical stage.

> Received a call reporting that _____, female adult, 18, had been pronounced dead in the Medical Intensive Care Unit by Dr. French at 13:59, May 30.
>
> The decedent had been taken to _____ Hospital by her father at 14:30, May 28, after collapsing while working in a cotton field. The exact location could not be determined. Upon arrival at the hospital, the decedent had a rectal temperature of 107.5 degrees Fahrenheit. She was given oxygen and packed in ice and by 15:10 her temperature had dropped to 103.5. She was suffering from seizures and a constant flow of yellow, watery diarrhea. She was unresponsive the entire time she was at the hospital and her pupils were three to four millimeters wide.
>
> She was transferred to the Medical Intensive Care Unit, where efforts were made to regulate her body temperature and it was reduced to 100.4 degrees Fahrenheit. The seizures continued, however, and she began to have myocardial and renal (heart and kidney) failure and disseminated intravascular coagulation (blood clots throughout her body). She was on dialysis when she died.
>
> The decedent's family reported that she had been working in the fields for three days prior to her collapse. She had taken a tylenol for a headache around noon, May 28, but immediately threw it up.
> The United States Weather Bureau reported that the high temperatures for May 25 through May 28 were 93, 96, 102, and 107 degrees Fahrenheit, respectively.[77]

---

[75]   United States Environmental Protection Agency, "A Guide to Heat Stress in Agriculture," EPA-750-b-92-001, May 1993, p. 1.

[76] Ibid.

[77] Ibid., p. 2.

Many of the young workers interviewed by Human Rights Watch had suffered from mild to moderate heat illness, with symptoms including dizziness, headaches, nausea, and vomiting.   Two reported witnessing cases of heat illness—one of a sister, another of a boyfriend—so severe that the afflicted person was unable to work for an entire week "He had the heat inside him," described one. "He was very pale and throwing up." "He was sick from the sun."[78]

Musculoskeletal Trauma

The strenuous and often awkward labor of farmwork increases the risk of injuries, including chronic repetitive stress disorders and musculoskeletal trauma. Several teens told Human Rights Watch that they suffered from chronic back and/or neck pain when they were working in the fields.

Early adolescence is a time of rapid growth, which makes teenage workers more vulnerable than adults to musculoskeletal disorders.[79] Agricultural work in particular has been linked to musculoskeletal trauma, due to the stresses on the body of constant bending, lifting, twisting, and other awkward or punishing work.[80] Furthermore, because back pain is generally rare among adolescents as a whole—and a history of back pain is a risk factor for new back injuries— medical experts conclude that "the long-term consequences of back strains among adolescent workers are of substantial concern."[81]

Carbon Monoxide Poisoning Incident in Washington State

On July 25, 1997, approximately one hundred workers were poisoned by carbon monoxide at a packing plant in Washington state. Seven of these workers were fifteen years old or younger and therefore underage for packing plant employment under Washington law.[82] Another ten were sixteen or

---

[78] Human Rights Watch interview with Jane T., October 27, 1998, Casa Grande, Arizona.

[79]   National Research Council and Institute of Medicine, *Protecting Youth at Work: Health, Safety, and Development of Working Children and Adolescents in the United States* (Washington, D.C.: National Academy Press, 1998), p. 93.

[80] See Ibid., p. 156.

[81] Ibid., p. 94.

[82] Human Rights Watch telephone interview with attorney involved in the case, who prefers to remain unnamed, March 9, 1999. Washington state has determined that packing shed employment is "particularly hazardous," and forbids employment of children under sixteen in packing sheds. This is more protective than federal law.

seventeen years old.[83] The youngest of the affected workers were fourteen years old.[84]

The doors to the packing room where the poisoning occurred were shut on the day of the poisoning. Two of the doors were taped shut with duct tape; two other doors were covered with fine mesh nets.[85] The ventilation fan was broken, and there were multiple sources of carbon monoxide in operation.[86]

A report by doctors from the Occupational and Environmental Medicine Clinic of Harborview Medical Center, University of Washington, estimated that workers' exposure levels to carbon monoxide on the day of the poisoning ranged between 200 and 500 parts per million.[87] The permissible exposure limit for carbon monoxide is 35 parts per million.[88]

Human Rights Watch interviewed Flor Trujillo (her real name), one of the affected workers. Flor was fifteen years old at the time of the poisoning.

I was working at the plant for two weeks before the poisoning. For the whole two weeks I was having headaches; by after lunch it would be pretty bad. I would ask my supervisor if she had anything for it and she would give me a packet of Pain-Aid pills—but then she said she couldn't give them to me anymore. I think because I was underage.

The last day me and my friend went to the little store and got pills because we had bad headaches. Everyone was like "me too," so I gave some other people some of the pills.

A couple of hours after lunch this girl who was working by us fainted. . . . A couple of hours later another girl fainted, a high school

---

[83] Human Rights Watch telephone interview with Flor Trujillo, underage victim of the mass poisoning, March 24, 1999.

[84] Center of Excellence for Chemically Related Illness, Harborview Occupational and Environmental Medicine Clinic, Harborview Medical Center, University of Washington, "Review of Claims Related to the Carbon Monoxide Incident at Brewster Heights Packing Inc.," February 12, 1998, University of Washington, Seattle, Washington, p. 7.

[85] Ibid., p. 6.

[86] Ibid.

[87] Ibid., p. 13.

[88] Ibid.

girl; she was probably sixteen. . . . After her then a bunch of people were fainting.

The manager told us to keep working, wouldn't let us leave. Finally our supervisor told us to leave. These kids [workers] were jumping on the doors to tear the tape off, open the doors so we could get outside. . . . I was all shaky and cold and trembling. I passed out.

It took about two weeks for me to start feeling better. I had bad headaches. I wanted to sleep all day. I was really weak.

I got a letter in the mail saying I couldn't work there anymore because I wasn't over sixteen years old. When we got the job they didn't ask how old we were.

I still get really bad headaches. They seem like a part of life now. They come every day. . . . I remember what happened and I feel really bad about what could have happened . . . That's the worst thing that's ever happened to me. It scared me a lot and still does. I'm scared of being in a place that's shut. . . . Sometimes I start crying because I still remember.[89]

The Harborview Medical Center report states that, "[g]iven the estimated exposures . . . it is not surprising that some workers have chronic complaints."[90]

Approximately one hundred workers were seen at the local hospital's emergency room on the day of the incident, with symptoms including dizziness, headaches, nausea, and loss of consciousness; ninety-three workers filed claims for carbon monoxide poisoning.[91] As a result of this mass poisoning, Washington's Department of Labor and Industries levied a fine against the company, Brewster Heights Packing, Inc., in the amount of two thousand dollars.[92]

---

[89] Human Rights Watch telephone interview, March 24, 1999.

[90] Harborview Medical Center, "Review of Claims," p. 5.

[91] Ibid., p. 2.

[92] Human Rights Watch telephone interview with attorney involved in the case, who prefers to remain unnamed, March 9, 1999.

Hazardous Equipment; Work-Related Injuries

In a Florida orange grove in January 1999, two young farmworkers fell off the tailgate of a moving pickup truck. Several crates of oranges fell on top of them, killing one of the boys and wounding the other. The boy who died, Miguel Angel Ramos, was either fourteen or fifteen years old; the other boy was fifteen. The accident occurred on a school day.[93]

Agriculture is the most dangerous occupation open to juveniles in the United States.[94] Farmworkers routinely use knives, hoes, and other cutting implements; operate or work near heavy machinery; work on ladders; and work with or near pesticides and other dangerous chemicals. Children working in agriculture in the U.S. make up only 8 percent of the population of working minors overall, yet account for 40 percent of work-related fatalities among minors.[95] An estimated 100,000 children suffer agriculture-related injuries annually in the United States.[96] Minors working in agriculture have also been found to suffer a higher frequency of severe and disabling injuries than those working in all other occupations.[97]

Daniel F., sixteen, described to Human Rights Watch an injury he suffered the previous year, when he was fifteen years old and working at a large hydroponic tomato nursery in Willcox, Arizona.[98]

---

[93] Association of Farmworker Opportunity Programs, "Child Dies in Orange Grove Accident," *Washington Newsline*, http://www.afop.org/newsletter/jan_feb99/kiddies.html.

[94] According to the National Safety Council, agriculture is second only to mining in occupational fatalities. Arroyo and Kurre, "Young Agricultural Workers in California," Labor Occupational Health Program, Center for Occupational and Environmental Health, School of Public Health, University of California, Berkeley, November 1997, pp. 23-24, citing National Safety Council, "Accident Facts," 1996. The Department of Labor prohibits employment of youth under the age of eighteen in mining.

[95] National Research Council and Institute of Medicine, *Protecting Youth at Work*, p. 153.

[96] Ibid.

[97] Arroyo and Kurre, "Young Agricultural Workers in California," p. 28, citing a study in Washington state.

[98] Human Rights Watch interview, Willcox, Arizona, March 16, 1999.

We were putting plastic on the ground, rolling it down off of big long rolls. There was a big hole in the floor. [As Daniel F. explained, this appears to have been the open end of a pipe, perpendicular to and flush with the floor.] I couldn't see it; it was covered with plastic. I stepped in it, fell in, whacked my knee.

Daniel F. underwent treatment for several months, including multiple visits to an orthopedic specialist, magnetic resonance imaging, and anti-inflammatory injections and pills. For two months he was on crutches; for three months he was in a knee brace.

The doctor said I will never be 100 percent cured. I can't play soccer anymore; before the accident I was in a league. I can't really play basketball. My knee still bothers me. For example, if I run it gives in . . . even if I walk sometimes it can do that.

The nursery paid for Daniel F.'s medical expenses and he received workers' compensation. But the company also sent him a letter to sign—a liability release, by his description—from their insurer.

Even at the age of fifteen, Daniel F.'s work at the nursery in the summer was legal—under current Arizona and federal law, hydroponic nurseries are not classified as hazardous workplaces. Daniel F. told Human Rights Watch of other injuries that occurred at the hydroponic nurseries, as did a legal aid attorney involved in several claims against Bonita. "They are taking farmworkers and having them do work they are not accustomed to. It is more heavily industrialized than farmwork, [with] trolleys going around the ceiling, big vats of water, people driving little carts. . . . These are not injuries a farmworker would look out for. That industry ought to be declared hazardous."[99]

Tractors and other motorized farm equipment represent very serious hazards, and the FLSA prohibits their operation by children aged fifteen and younger. Abidance by this prohibition, and enforcement when it is violated, is another matter. Human Rights Watch interviewed a sixteen-year old who had worked full time for the three previous summers—when thirteen, fourteen, and fifteen years old—driving a tractor.

Even those not operating farm equipment themselves may be in danger. According to Art Morelos of the Industrial Commission of Arizona, "a common

---

[99] Human Rights Watch telephone interview with Gary Restaino, then-staff attorney for Community Legal Services Farmworker Program, Phoenix, Arizona, April 26, 1999.

safety hazard in cantaloupe and lettuce fields, where the packing is done in the field, is that the tractor will be set to move without a driver. It goes very slowly, but is still dangerous."[100] In fact, it can be deadly, as illustrated by the incident noted earlier in this chapter, in which a drunken seventeen-year reportedly fell in front of a cantaloupe packing tractor and was killed.

For all workers, but especially for field workers, fatigue increases the risk of injury.   Long hours, early morning hours, and work in very hot conditions all increase fatigue, as does the heavy physical labor entailed in most agricultural work. The relative inexperience of young workers also increases their risk of accidents and injury.

Cuts from knives were the injury most commonly reported to Human Rights Watch by young workers.   Several knew of other people who had been injured badly, their fingers cut off by knives or their hands mangled in machinery.

A boy working in the Yuma area told Human Rights Watch of a knife injury he suffered when he was fifteen years old.[101] He cut his finger with a broccoli-harvesting knife.   "That knife was so sharp," he said, showing his finger with a curved scar about three inches long running the length of it.

The field supervisor did not have a first-aid kit—only Band-Aids. According to the boy's older sister, the cut was bad and needed medical attention.[102] However, because her brother was both underage (at fifteen, he was too young to be working legally during school hours) and undocumented, he was not taken to a local hospital or clinic. Instead, he was taken across the border to his parents' house in Mexico and from there to a Mexican hospital, where he received multiple stitches. The delay from the time of the injury to the time of treatment was between two and three hours.

Advocates and workers report that it is typical for injured workers to go to Mexico for treatment, for a variety of reasons. The employer may want to avoid workers' compensation claims in order to keep their rates low. The worker may be undocumented and afraid of discovery, or afraid they will be denied treatment at a clinic or hospital in the United States. In addition, health care services for farmworkers are often very far away and difficult to access.

---

[100] Human Rights Watch interview with Compliance Supervisor Art Morelos, Tucson, Arizona, October 15, 1998.

[101] Human Rights Watch interview with Benjamin C., Somerton, Arizona, October 1, 1998.

[102] Human Rights Watch interview with Damaris A., Somerton, Arizona, October 1, 1998.

Depression and Substance Abuse

Farmworkers in general have high rates of depression.[103] Extreme poverty and hardship, the stress of job uncertainty and frequent moves, and social stigmatization and isolation are contributing factors. This is true for children and youth as well. Studies have also linked depression in teenage workers to long hours of work in high-intensity, low-skilled jobs—precisely the kind of labor undertaken by farmworkers.[104]

As a result of these pressures, farmworkers are vulnerable to substance abuse, which can alleviate pain and offer a temporary escape from difficult lives. In addition, though, some substance abuse is directly related to work. This includes not just the unsafe practice, encouraged by some avaricious employers, of drinking beer sold at the work site. It also includes drugs taken for the express purpose of getting more work done.

Some farmworker youth use drugs "in order to fulfill the demands of work," according to Emma Torres, a former farmworker who now coordinates a border health and substance abuse prevention project in the Yuma area.[105] This is particularly true for boys and young men working at the piece rate, where the pace at which one works directly determines earnings. "They use speed to make it through the day," says Torres.[106]

> The farmworker is like a machine: the harder they work the more they will earn. So they push their body to the max. That's why they do drugs—not to feel high, but with the purpose of extracting more work from their body . . . But the body can only take so much, and after a few years they end up disabled, young, and on the street, begging. They don't qualify for Social Security, they have no insurance . . . but their hands or backs don't work anymore.[107]

---

[103] National Center for Farmworker Health, "Who are America's Farmworkers?" p. 6.

[104] National Research Council and Institute of Medicine, *Protecting Youth at Work*, p. 131.

[105] Human Rights Watch telephone interview with Emma Torres, Project Coordinator, Bridges in Friendship (a project of the Border Health Foundation), Somerton, Arizona, October 19, 1998.

[106] Human Rights Watch interview with Emma Torres, Somerton, Arizona, September 30, 1998.

[107] Human Rights Watch telephone interview with Emma Torres, October 19, 1998.

Underage Workers

No one ever cared how old I was.
—Ricky N., who began working in the fields at the age of fourteen.[108]

"Underage worker" is a slippery concept in agriculture, as children are legally permitted to work at very young ages. Under certain not-too-rigorous circumstances, federal and most state laws permit children as young as twelve to work for hire in agriculture, an age far younger than that permitted in other occupations. Under more limited conditions, even children aged ten and eleven can work as hired farm laborers.

Enforcement of these laws, weak as they are, is lax. Growers and farm labor contractors frequently hire underage workers, a category that includes children under the age of sixteen working during school hours, children aged thirteen or younger working without parental consent, and children under the age of sixteen who engage in hazardous agricultural tasks.

State laws regarding the minimum age of employment as a hired farmworker vary widely. According to a 1997 survey by the Child Labor Coalition, eighteen states have no minimum age requirement for children working in agriculture.[109] In Oregon, the minimum age is nine; in Illinois it is ten.[110] Fourteen states require a minimum age of twelve; in nine states the minimum age is fourteen.[111] Only one state, Nevada, has set sixteen as the minimum age for hired farmworkers.

The Fair Labor Standards Act (FLSA) sets the federal minimum age for child labor. (Whichever legal standard—state or federal—is most stringent is the one that applies.) The Fair Labor Standards Act dates back to 1938 and reflects a radically different era in the United States, a time when "agriculture" was

---

[108] Human Rights Watch interview, Casa Grande, Arizona, October 27, 1998.

[109] These states are Alabama, Arizona, Delaware, Kentucky, Louisiana, Maine, Massachusetts, Michigan, Nebraska, New Hampshire, North Carolina, North Dakota, Oklahoma, South Dakota, Tennessee, Texas, Utah, and Wyoming. Child Labor Coalition, "1997 Child Labor State Survey," National Consumers League, Washington, DC, 1997, p. 12. The Child Labor Coalition conducts a state child labor survey every two years.

[110] Ibid.

[111] States with a twelve-year minimum age requirement are Arkansas, Georgia, Idaho, Indiana, Kansas, Maryland, Minnesota, New Jersey, New York, South Carolina, Virginia, Washington, and Wisconsin. Those with a fourteen-year minimum age requirement are Alaska, California, Connecticut, Hawaii, Missouri, Montana, New Mexico, Rhode Island, and West Virginia. Ibid.

synonymous with "family farm," and a quarter of all Americans still lived and worked on farms. Initially, farmworkers were excluded entirely from the law's protection, and restrictions on child labor in agriculture were not added until 1974.

The law is woefully inadequate to protect today's hired farmworkers, who are overwhelmingly employed as wage laborers in commercial enterprises, and not on the family farm, including the hundreds of thousands of workers aged seventeen and under. The FLSA standards differ between agricultural and nonagricultural work. Employment of children thirteen or younger is forbidden in nonagricultural occupations. Children aged fourteen and fifteen may work in nonagricultural settings for limited hours outside of school: up to three hours on a school day; up to eighteen hours in a school week; up to eight hours on a nonschool day; and up to forty hours in a nonschool week. They may not work before 7 a.m. or after 7 p.m. (9 p.m. in the summer). Youth sixteen and older may work in any nonhazardous nonagricultural occupation.[112]

For children working in agriculture, the FLSA is much less protective. Children younger than twelve may work unlimited hours outside of school, if this work takes place on a small farm with a parent's written consent.[113] Children aged twelve and thirteen may work unlimited hours outside of school on any farm with written parental consent, or without written consent on a farm where a parent is employed.[114] Children aged fourteen and fifteen may work unlimited hours outside of school on any farm, without parental consent.[115] There are no hourly restrictions on the agricultural work of children who are sixteen or older.

In addition to allowing agricultural employers to employ children for longer hours and at younger ages, the FLSA also permits sixteen and seventeen-year olds to engage in *hazardous* agricultural work.[116] In other occupational settings, eighteen is the minimum age for hazardous work.

---

[112] 29 U.S.C. section 213.

[113] 29 U.S.C. section 213(c)(1)(A). A "small farm" is one which did not employ more than 500 man-days of agricultural labor during any calendar quarter of the preceding year. 29 U.S.C. section 213(a). Five hundred man-days would typically be reached by seven employees working six days a week during a calendar quarter. Human Rights Watch telephone interview with Gary Restaino, then-staff attorney with Community Legal Services Farmworker Program, April 26, 1999.

[114] 29 U.S.C. section 213(c)(1)(B).

[115] 29 U.S.C. section 213(c)(1)(C).

[116] 29 U.S.C. section 213(c)(2).

Under federal law, then, it is legal for a twelve-year old child to harvest asparagus from 3 a.m. to 8 a.m. seven days a week, bending over in the pre-dawn cold and wielding a knife, then stumbling on to school. The same child would be prohibited from working in any nonagricultural work (other than wreath-making or newspaper delivery). A fifteen-year old may work fifty hours a week during the school year if she works in agriculture, but only eighteen hours a week if she works at Burger King.

Many of the youth interviewed by Human Rights Watch had dropped out of school before the age of sixteen in order to work full time in the fields. Employment of these children violated the law. Although federal law permits children to perform farmwork for unlimited hours outside of school, it does not permit the employment of children aged fifteen and under during school hours.

In most cases, children told Human Rights Watch that they were not asked their age prior to employment. When they were asked their ages, and/or to show proof of age, the fact that they were under sixteen did not deter the farm labor contractors or growers from hiring them anyway. All of the juveniles believed their employers knew them to be underage.

Jessica G., for example, left school two years ago at the age of fifteen to work in the melon fields near Yuma, where the season runs from November to April.[117] She worked from 4:00 a.m. until 3:00 or 4:00 p.m.—an eleven or twelve-hour day. She earned $36 a day; at about $3 an hour, well below minimum wage. "It's very difficult work," she said. "You're outside all day, with just a couple of short breaks." "I was very tired at the end of the day." Both the manager of the farm and the farm labor contractor who hired Jessica G. were friends of her family. Four of the five children in Jessica G.'s family have worked in the fields. Their grandmother raised them, as their mother always worked in the fields as well.

Richard M. told Human Rights Watch about his first agricultural job, when he was fourteen.

> As long as you're fifteen you can get a job. My uncle drives you to the field and tells the contractor he has a new worker. He'll put you on the payroll. . . . They do ask to see your social security and your birth certificate. When I was fourteen I showed them my social security and my birth certificate. . . . Yeah, I wasn't old enough to work out there.   —Richard M., seventeen years old[118]

---

[117] Human Rights Watch interview with Jessica G., Somerton, Arizona, September 30, 1998.

[118] Human Rights Watch interview, Casa Grande, Arizona, October 27, 1998.

But Richard M. did work at that field, until he got sick two weeks later from pesticide poisoning.

Blanca Rodriguez, now an attorney working with farmworkers in Washington state, recalls working in the asparagus fields with her parents from the age of five or six on. The asparagus harvest generally runs from April through June, coinciding with the last portion of the school year.

> We'd get up at 2:00 a.m., go to the fields, and then go to school. That's why parents do it, because they can still send their kids to school. And in high school we would stay a bit later with our parents, then go to night school. The high school still has a night school option for asparagus cutters during the season.[119]

According to Rodriguez, children as young as ten and eleven still work in the asparagus fields. Not all go to school at the same time; some drop out for the season, or drop out for the asparagus season and stay out for the summer and early fall, until the apple harvest ends in October.[120]

In two cases looked at by Human Rights Watch, underage workers were badly injured on the job; in one of these, the worker was subsequently denied compensation and fired for being underage. The case of Flor Trujillo (her real name) is described more fully in the chapter titled "Health and Safety Risks." Trujillo was hired at the age of fifteen to work in a fruit-packing plant in central Washington state. Under Washington law, work in a packing plant is considered hazardous, and workers must be at least sixteen years of age. At the time she was hired, Trujillo was not asked her age. A few weeks later, she and about one hundred of her co-workers were poisoned by carbon-monoxide fumes inside the plant. Seven of the poisoned workers were fifteen or younger. Within a month of the incident, Trujillo received a letter from the company, Brewster Heights Packing, Inc., telling her that she could no longer work there because she was underage. Trujillo did not receive any compensation from the company for the danger in which it placed her, her resulting illness, or her lost income.[121]

In Willcox, Arizona, a fifteen-year old boy suffered a permanently-disabling injury to his knee while working at Bonita Nurseries, a Dutch-owned

---

[119] Human Rights Watch telephone interview with Blanca Rodriguez, attorney with the United Farm Workers, Sunnyside, WA, March 10, 1999.

[120] Ibid.

[121] Human Rights Watch telephone interview with Flor Trujillo, March 24, 1999.

hydroponic tomato nursery. This case is discussed further in the chapter "Health and Safety Risks."

Frank M., a boy interviewed in central Arizona, began working in 1996, the summer he was thirteen. His job was to drive a tractor up and down dirt roads, wetting the roads so the dust wouldn't fly in the face of the workers. He said he drove at about 25 miles per hour.[122]

Under the FLSA, driving a tractor or other farm vehicle is considered hazardous, and therefore prohibited for any juvenile under the age of sixteen. "It was under the table until last year, when the boss put me on the payroll," said Frank M.. "He knew how old I was."[123]

Not only was Frank M. working illegally, but his employer was underpaying him too, giving him one hundred dollars a week for roughly a forty-hour work week; in other words, about $2.50 an hour—just over half of the minimum wage at that time.

Other boys also told Human Rights Watch about their early years of work:

I worked the cotton fields starting when I was twelve, weeding with a hoe between the plants. I worked from 4:00 a.m. to 2:00 p.m. [ten hours], with a thirty minute break for lunch. You just go up and down the rows. There were lots of kids out there, twelve, thirteen years old.
—Mark H., nineteen[124]

Mark H.—working ten hours a day at the age of twelve in the cotton fields of central Arizona, where the temperature routinely rises above 110 degrees— was working with his parents' knowledge. His aunt, a friend of the grower, had gotten him his job. Because the work took place during the summer, and therefore outside of school hours, and because he worked on a small farm, the fact of his employment was, for the most part, perfectly legal (with the exception that his parents had not provided written consent regarding their son's employment). In violation of the FLSA, he was paid below minimum wage, earning only about $3.50 an hour. He was paid under the table, without Social Security deductions being made on his behalf, also an illegal practice. Yet in the four years that Mark H. worked summers in the field, to his knowledge not a single state or federal authority ever checked on his employer's practices.

---

[122] Human Rights Watch interview, Casa Grande, Arizona, October 27, 1998.

[123] Ibid.

[124] Human Rights Watch interview, Casa Grande, Arizona, November 3, 1998.

I pitched watermelons. Now that's some hard work. You throw it down the line, one to the other, standing about five feet apart.

That's when I was fourteen. I worked pitching watermelons from about 4:00 to 8:00 p.m. Because in the morning I was doing other work. I chopped cotton from four or five in the morning until noon. Then they make you go home and rest. Then watermelon.

So it was like, eight hours in the morning, then four hours at night. Cotton and watermelon is hard work. I'd get home about eight, go to sleep around ten, then get up at four. . . . It's hard. You can faint. You have to drink lots of water.

—Dean S., sixteen years old[125]

Dean S. worked twelve hours a day at the age of fourteen, sleeping only six hours a night. He chopped cotton and pitched watermelons, both difficult and exhausting forms of work with a high risk of injury. The fact of his summer employment was entirely legal, however—as a fourteen year old, employers could hire him for farmwork without any hourly restrictions whatsoever, except that he not work during school hours.

Wage and Hour Concerns

Wage Fraud: Earning Less than Minimum Wage

With some exceptions, juvenile farmworkers are entitled by law to earn the prevailing minimum wage.[126] Since September 1, 1997, the federal minimum wage has been $5.15 per hour. (As of this writing in late 1999, members of Congress are discussing a rise in the minimum wage.) From October 1, 1996 to August 31, 1997, the minimum hourly wage was $4.75; from April 1, 1991 to October 1, 1996, the federal minimum wage was $4.25. In those states with a

---

[125] Human Rights Watch interview, Casa Grande, Arizona, November 3, 1998.

[126] The minimum wage requirements of the Fair Labor Standards Act do not apply to: (1) farmworkers, including minors, whose employers used less than 500 man-days of farm labor during every calendar quarter of the previous year; (2) non-migrant hand-harvest laborers who are paid on a piece-rate basis and who worked in agriculture less than thirteen weeks the previous year; and (3) workers sixteen years of age and younger who are employed at the same farm as their parent and who are hand-harvest laborers paid at a piece rate. 29 C.F.R. 780.300.

higher minimum wage—Washington voters, for example, approved a minimum wage of $5.75 in 1998—employers must pay the state-mandated minimum wage.

Agricultural employers may pay either an hourly rate or a piece-rate. If they pay by a piece-rate, the earnings for all hours worked in a work week must be sufficient to bring the average hourly wage up to at least minimum wage.[127]

Depending on the speed, skill, and strength of the worker—and the worker's co-workers, if he or she is working as part of a team—piece-rate wages can be either beneficial or problematic. The strongest, fastest, and most experienced workers can earn in excess of minimum wage (although usually not above $7.00 or $7.50 per hour). Slower or weaker workers, or those just starting out in agriculture, may earn less than half of minimum wage. Adolescents can fall into either one of these two groups, although it is usually only older adolescents, often male, who excel at piece-rate work. Success at piece-rate work, however, can carry an additional price in terms of its toll on the body.[128]

Approximately one-third of the juveniles interviewed by Human Rights Watch reported earning significantly less than minimum wage. Most of these teens worked for small growers. Not all were paid by an hourly minimum wage or by piece-rate—several were paid instead a fixed lump sum per day or per week.

These findings comport with those of a recent National Agricultural Workers Survey, which found that agricultural workers aged fourteen through seventeen earned just over $4 an hour, on average.[129] The Department of Labor's Wage and Hour Division has also reported high rates of wage fraud, with more than half of grape growers and farm labor contractors surveyed found to be violating minimum wage requirements.[130]

The following are some examples of the experiences of adolescent farmworkers paid by both the piece-rate and lump-sum method:

---

[127] Unless the worker falls under one of the exempt categories; see preceding footnote.

[128] See the chapter "Health and Safety Risks" regarding cumulative injuries and substance abuse.

[129] Cited in U.S. General Accounting Office, "Child Labor in Agriculture: Characteristics and Legality of Work," Washington, D.C.: U.S. General Accounting Office, 1998; GAO/HEHS-98-112R, p. 7.

[130] U.S. Department of Labor, "Compliance Highlights: 1998 Agricultural Activity Report, Wage and Hour Division," March 1999, p. 2 (regarding California findings); U.S. Department of Labor Wage and Hour Division, Phoenix District Memorandum, "Phoenix District Grape Survey," November 10, 1998 (regarding Arizona findings). The Department of Labor surveys did not distinguish between juvenile and adult workers.

- In 1998, Sani H., then sixteen, picked chilies at the rate of fifty cents per bag (about the size of a bushel). He worked from 7:00 a.m. until 3:00 p.m. and earned about $20 a day, for an average hourly wage of $2.50.[131]

- In 1996, John P., then fifteen, picked apples for piece-rate wages. He worked ten hours a day—from 5:00 a.m. until 3:00 p.m.—and earned between twenty and thirty dollars a day ($2 to $3 an hour). Two years later, in 1998, he picked cherries, again working ten-hour days. For that work he was paid $42 a day, or just over $4 an hour—one dollar less per hour than minimum wage. This means that John P., who worked Monday through Friday and a half-day on Saturday, was shortchanged $55 a week by his employer.[132]

- Mark H. worked every summer from the age of twelve to sixteen in the cotton fields south of Phoenix. He usually worked from 4:00 a.m. until 2:00 p.m. (ten hours), six days a week. The last summer he worked this job, in 1996, the farmer he worked for paid him a flat weekly rate of $200—about $3.50 an hour, well below minimum wage at that time.[133]

- In 1997, when he was fourteen years old, Dean S. worked twelve hours a day for a local farmer: eight hours in the morning in the cotton fields and four hours in the evening pitching watermelon. The most he ever earned was $50 a day, or about $4 an hour.[134]
- Ricky N., who also pitched watermelon in central Arizona, earned between $2.75 and $3.00 an hour in 1996, when he was fifteen. The federal minimum wage was then $4.25 an hour.[135]

- When Jessica G. was fifteen, in 1996, she worked in the cantaloupe fields of southwestern Arizona for eleven to twelve hours each day. Each day, she was allowed one fifteen-minute break in the morning and

---

[131] Human Rights Watch interview, Willcox, Arizona, March 16, 1999.

[132] Human Rights Watch interview, Willcox, Arizona, March 16, 1999.

[133] Human Rights Watch interview, Casa Grande, Arizona, November 3, 1998.

[134] Ibid.

[135] Human Rights Watch interview, Casa Grande, Arizona, October 27, 1998.

one thirty-minute break for lunch. She earned $36 a day—about $3 an hour, which was approximately 65 percent of the minimum wage at that time.[136]

In violation of the FLSA, none of the employers in the above cases provided additional compensation to bring their workers' wages up to the legal hourly minimum. None of these young workers knew they had been cheated of their rightful wages.

The above examples involved juvenile workers on relatively small farms or working for small-scale farm labor contractors. Underpayment of wages, however, is by no means limited to small growers or farm labor contractors. Human Rights Watch interviewed two young women who had previously worked for a major agribusiness. Both of them reported that they—and their co-workers—had been routinely cheated on their pay.

They take hours away from your pay. This is very common—they short all the workers. Almost always, every check, they cut off a little bit. Like, let's say you work eighty hours—they'll pay you for seventy. So you end up making less than minimum wage.[137]

According to the girls, the amount cut out of the pay varied from check to check, but the practice was consistent.

Another thing they do is, sometimes when you're supposed to work eight hours, for example, they make you work more but still pay only for eight.[138]

Asked if they had ever complained about these practices, the girls said no. "Some of the workers complained but it did no good," they said. They told Human Rights Watch that they believed they had no recourse. Practically speaking, they did not. Their employer was one of a handful of large corporate growers operating on state-owned land in western Arizona. The nearest town to the fields the girls were working in is Wendon, with a population of 450, and the nearest enforcement agency offices—the Department of Labor's Wage and Hour Division and the State of Arizona Industrial Commission—are in Phoenix, two

---

[136] Human Rights Watch interview, Somerton, Arizona, October 1, 1998.

[137] Human Rights Watch interviews with Sylvia R. and Dina V., Aguila, Arizona, April 9, 1999.

[138] Ibid.

hours away. Nor is there public bus service to Wendon, Aguila, Salome, or any of the other tiny towns in that vast and isolated area west of Phoenix.

The girls said they had once seen a government inspector—for which agency they did not know. They had been prompted on more than one occasion by their supervisors, however, who told them what to say if approached by a government official: "If they ask how much I pay you, say $5.50," or "say $6.00," they told us. "And so that's what people would say . . . . There are a lot of unfair practices."[139]

Excessive and Inappropriate Hours of Work

In contrast to nonagricultural occupations, the FLSA imposes neither a daily nor a weekly limit to the number of hours children may work in agriculture. Human Rights Watch spoke with several adolescent farmworkers who worked twelve hours a day for six or six and a half days a week, and a few who had worked fourteen hours a day or more.

> We would work as much as was needed. You could work up to fourteen or fifteen hours a day. But you're not forced to work more than twelve; beyond twelve is optional.
>
> —Frank M., sixteen, describing the hours he worked the summer he was fifteen, in Avondale, Arizona[140]

Under current law there is nothing illegal about employers extracting such long hours from children, unless the work occurs during school hours and the children are under sixteen.

Damaris A., a legal permanent resident of the United States, worked in the fields near Yuma, Arizona from the age of thirteen until she was seventeen. Despite her and her family's right to reside in the United States, a severe housing shortage in the Yuma area prevented them from doing so. Instead, like thousands of others, Damaris A., her younger brother, and her father crossed into the U.S. each day from the city of San Luís Río Colorado, Mexico, into the town of San Luis, Arizona. From there, the workers are driven by bus or truck to work sites near and far.

In order to get to work by 7:00 a.m., Damaris A. would rise at 3:00 a.m., prepare for work, then wait about two hours to cross the international port of

---

[139] Ibid.

[140] Human Rights Watch interview, Casa Grande, Arizona, October 27, 1998.

entry. The wait was due to the long lines of people crossing through, like Damaris A., to go to work in the fields on the U.S. side. During the peak season, immigration officials estimate that more than 6,000 farmworkers cross the border daily at the San Luis, Arizona port of entry.[141] The majority of these workers are, like Damaris A., legal permanent residents of the United States.[142]

Once on the U.S. side, Damaris A. still had to travel to the work site, which could take up to two hours depending on the location of the fields where the farm labor contractor had her crew working.

The peak season for lettuce and cantaloupe in the Yuma area runs from April to November. During the height of the season, Damaris A. worked from 7 a.m. until 9 p.m., six days a week. Occasionally she worked a half-day on Sunday as well. During her fourteen-hour workdays, she was permitted two fifteen-minute breaks and a half-hour for lunch. She earned minimum wage. Some weeks, she worked as many as ninety hours.

At night, Damaris A. would reverse the travel process she had undertaken in the morning: travel to the border crossing, wait two hours or so to complete the crossing, and finally arrive home by midnight. On her busiest days, then, Damaris A. had only three hours of sleep at home before starting all over again in the morning.

This was illegal employment—for three years, Damaris A. was under sixteen and working during school hours. She got her job through her father, who worked for the same grower and was friendly with the foreman. Damaris A. lied about her age and was hired despite producing no documentation of her birth date.

Another young worker, Gerardo L., worked in the melon fields near El Centro, California, when he was seventeen. His work was not illegal—he was old enough to be working full time without restrictions—but it was long and grueling. He worked from 5:00 a.m. until anywhere between noon and 8:00 p.m., depending on the needs of the grower. For one month during the peak harvest, he worked from 5:00 a.m. until 8:00 p.m., seven days a week—105 hours a week. He also had to travel one hour each way to and from work. He was paid minimum wage.[143]

---

[141] Carol Mell, "Keepers of the Green: Workers from Mexico fuel Yuma County's agriculture industry," *The Yuma Daily Sun,* http://www.yumasun.com/news/index.shtml.

[142] Ibid., quoting Mike Valadez, Immigration and Naturalization Service Assistant Port Director for San Luis, Arizona.

[143] Human Rights Watch interview, Casa Grande, Arizona, November 3, 1998.

The Effect of Long Hours on Health and Education

Work in excess of twenty hours per week has a substantial and well-documented negative impact on teenagers' health, social development, and education. These issues are discussed further in the chapters on health and education.

The Effect of Farmwork on Education

All of the juvenile farmworkers interviewed by Human Rights Watch had dropped out of school or been held back at least one time. Nationally, the dropout rate for farmworker youth is 45 percent.[144] Reflecting this legacy of under-education, a full 80 percent of adult migrant farmworkers function at a 5th-grade literacy level or less.[145]

Several factors contribute to this lack of educational attainment among farmworker youth. Mobility, poverty, and the strain of too many hours of work—all three often the defining characteristics of farm work—are particularly detrimental for children and adolescents in school.

The necessary mobility of many farmworker families, as they follow the growing cycles of various crops in various locales, brings with it frequent and repeated changes in school. Not only does this interrupt learning, but it also makes it difficult for children to adapt socially to the school environment, and for teachers to teach effectively. According to the National Center for Farmworker Health, changing schools takes an emotional toll on children, who are more likely to drop out if they change schools four or more times.[146]

The extreme poverty of their families means that many farmworker children and youth do not have the option of going to school—their families cannot afford for them to study, either because there is not enough money for shoes and clothes or because the children are themselves required to work. "A lot of kids don't even go to school anymore," an outreach worker told Human Rights Watch. "They never get caught because they move around. Their

---

[144] United States General Accounting Office, "Hired Farmworkers: Health and Well-Being at Risk," Washington, D.C.: U.S. General Accounting Office, 1992; GAO/HRD-092-46, p. 37. Among non-farmworkers, the dropout rate is only 29 percent. Ibid.

[145] Diane Mull, "U.S. Farmworker Children Lack Needed Workplace Protection," *Youth Advocate Program International Report*, vol. 3, no. 1, Spring 1998, p. 3, (citing U.S. Department of Education, "The Education of Adult Migrant Farmworkers," vol. 2, 1991).

[146] National Center for Farmworker Health, "Who are America's Farmworkers?" http://www.ncfh.org/aboutfws/aboutfws.htm, p. 7.

families aren't emphasizing education. They say, "We need to live day by day; you need to get out there and earn some money."[147]

One of the most significant causes of low educational achievement is the fact that juvenile farmworkers simply spend too much time on the job. Numerous studies have found that long hours of work—generally defined as twenty or more hours a week during the school year—interfere with scholastic performance.[148] In addition to not having time to study, students who engage in so-called "high intensity work" (again, work of twenty or more hours a week) generally don't get enough sleep, sleeping only seven hours a night rather than the nine they need.[149] As a result, these worker-students are sleepy during school (and on the job, which leads to higher rates of injury), more likely to be tardy or absent, and more likely to fall asleep in class.[150] Their excessive sleepiness interferes with learning; it may also contribute to emotional difficulties.[151] Finally, students working twenty or more hours a week are more likely to use stimulants—including caffeine—to compensate for their tiredness.[152]

Statistics are not available regarding the number of juvenile farmworkers working twenty or more hours a week. Anecdotal evidence, including Human Rights Watch findings, suggests that the majority of young farmworkers working during the school year are putting in work weeks of at least twenty hours and often more. A 1992 study found that, nationally, approximately 37 percent of adolescent farmworkers work full time.[153]

The United States Department of Labor (DOL) has never had statutory authority to limit the number of hours that sixteen and seventeen-year olds may work during the school year. Citing "the extensive research about the adverse effects of high-intensity work while school is in session," the National Research

---

[147] Human Rights Watch telephone interview with Amelia Lopez, former Arizona Department of Economic Security outreach worker, March 18, 1999.

[148] See generally National Research Council, *Protecting Youth at Work*, chapter five, "Work's Effect on Children and Adolescents," and in particular pp. 115-120.

[149] National Research Council, *Protecting Youth at Work*, p. 96.

[150] Ibid., p. 97.

[151] Ibid.

[152] Ibid.

[153] Arroyo and Kurre, "Young Agricultural Workers in California," Labor Occupational Health Program, Center for Occupational and Environmental Health, School of Public Health, University of California, Berkeley, November 1997, p. 31, citing a 1992 United States Department of Agriculture study.

Council recommended in 1998 that Congress provide DOL with the necessary authority to impose such limits.[154] In doing so, the council noted that:

> [T]he historical reasons that justified the exemption of those 16 and older from the hour limitation no longer apply. Furthermore, high-intensity work . . . has been associated with unhealthy and problem behaviors, including substance use and minor deviance, insufficient sleep and exercise, and limited time spent with families, and it is associated with decreased eventual educational attainment.[155]

In agriculture the situation is much worse, as there is no hourly restriction for *any* children working during the school year. Even children as young as twelve may legally work any number of hours during the week, regardless of the damage done to their health, their studies, and their overall well-being.[156]

Special Risks to Girls

Young female farmworkers face additional pressures and concerns, including frequent subjection to sexual harassment, discussed below. Children of farmworkers, and especially girls, often are responsible for significant duties in the home—caring for younger siblings, grocery shopping and food preparation, laundry, and housecleaning. Even for those who do not work yet in the fields, these responsibilities take the place of necessary study and sleep time, increasing the chances that they will drop out of school. "Instead of doing homework, they are caring for their baby brothers and sisters and taking care of the house. That's where [the family's poverty] is hurting them," according to Raúl Redondo, an outreach worker in Yuma, Arizona.[157] In addition, farmworker girls and young women have very high pregnancy rates. In Yuma

---

[154] National Research Council, *Protecting Youth at Work*, p. 11.

[155] Ibid.

[156] As previously noted, the National Research Council has addressed this disparity, recommending that the distinction between agricultural and nonagricultural occupations be eliminated, and that the more stringent nonagricultural restrictions apply to all working children. It should also be noted that, technically, children aged ten and eleven may also work as hired farmworkers under a special waiver system administered by the U.S. Department of Labor. As a practical matter, however, the issuance of such waivers has stopped or occurs on a very rare basis.

[157] Human Rights Watch interview, Yuma, Arizona, September 30, 1998.

County, where agriculture is the primary occupation, the teen pregnancy rate is 85.2 per 1,000; [158] the U.S. average, in contrast, is 54.4 per 1,000. [159]

Sexual Harassment

Sexual harassment of female workers is a top concern of farmworker advocates. Due to various factors, farmworker girls and women are exceptionally vulnerable to sexual harassment and assault. They work in isolated areas in a male-dominated occupation—female crew leaders and supervisors are unheard of—where education regarding sexual harassment is in its infancy. Often, they do not speak English, do not know that sexual harassment is illegal, and in any case have no one to turn to for help. Many of them are undocumented—that is, they have no legal status allowing them to be in the United States—and therefore are even more hesitant to report the harassment.

According to several advocates interviewed by Human Rights Watch, girls and women are subjected routinely to sexual advances by farm labor contractors and field supervisors. If they refuse, they—and members of their family—face retaliation in the form of discharge, blacklisting, and even physical assault and rape.

Two girls picking cantaloupes for a prominent agribusiness told Human Rights Watch that they had been sexually harassed by their respective supervisors. Co-workers also harassed one of the girls. Both were embarrassed in speaking about this and reluctant to provide details. One of the girls, though, gave the following account of harassment she experienced the previous summer, when she was seventeen.

> This supervisor, he was about forty-five years old, he was telling me sexual stuff. He said it in a serious way; I felt threatened. One time he told me to go with him to get ice, in his pickup. . . . on the way he asked me to go out with him. I told him no. "Why not?" he asked. He kept asking me questions, trying to talk me into it. For weeks he kept asking me. There was no one to complain to.

—Sylvia R., eighteen years old[160]

---

[158] L. Anne Newell, "State, Pima show better rates of teen pregnancy," *Arizona Daily Star*, April 6, 1999. The rates are for girls 15 to 19-years old.

[159] Patricia Donovan, "Falling Teen Pregnancy, Birthrates: What's Behind the Declines?" *The Guttmacher Report on Public Policy*, vol. I, no. 5, October 1998 (http://206.215.210.5/pubs/journals/gr010506.html).

These girls, who worked in a remote area two hours west of Phoenix, reported that sexual harassment of young farmworker women was common. Furthermore, both had heard reports of women being attacked, and both said they knew a local woman who had been raped by her supervisor. "He always insisted on giving her a ride home, and she ended up raped," said Sylvia R.. "That happens." Human Rights Watch asked Sylvia R. if anything happened to the man. "No," she replied. "He's the boss."

Human Rights Watch interviewed a woman in Yuma—not a minor—who said she was fired after resisting a sexual assault by her supervisor.

> One day my supervisor saw me downtown and offered me a ride home. How could I say no? He's my supervisor! I know his wife! . . . But when we got to my house he tried to come inside. He said "Oh, María, I want you so much!" and grabbed my breasts. I pushed him off me! I was shocked!
>
> The next morning when I got to work I was told to go home—they said there was nothing for me. I asked why. They said the supervisor didn't want me there anymore. After three years!
>
> —María, mid-fifties[161]

Although any woman working in the fields or the packing sheds is vulnerable to such abuse, young women are thought to be at an even higher risk for sexual assault and harassment. "Young women are particularly vulnerable," said Cindy O'Hara, a trial attorney with the Equal Employment Opportunity Commission (EEOC) in San Francisco.[162] "It's often the first job they've had, and they're not equipped to deal with [the harassment]. They don't have a lot of experience. A lot have just recently immigrated and gotten jobs. They feel they don't have a lot of options. Many of them are single parents."[163]

Sexual harassment in agriculture is particularly difficult to combat. As noted, the victims of the harassment often live and work in geographically

---

[160] Human Rights Watch interview, Aguila, Arizona, April 29, 1999.

[161] Human Rights Watch interview, Yuma, Arizona, September 30, 1998.

[162] The Equal Employment Opportunity Commission is a federal agency charged with enforcing federal civil rights laws as they relate to employment.

[163] Human Rights Watch telephone interview, May 5, 1999.

remote and isolated areas, may not speak English, and usually do not know that they have any legal recourse against the abuse. Culturally, they may be embarrassed to talk about it, according to O'Hara. They also may face anger from husbands or boyfriends who accuse them of encouraging or enjoying the harassing behavior. "There is a lot of guilt and anxiety [among harassment victims]," said O'Hara. "They think, 'What did I do to bring this on?' and become afraid to work, afraid it will happen again."

The most pressing deterrent to coming forward with a complaint is the fear of losing their job. As eighteen-year-old Sylvia R. told us, "Everyone is scared to say anything because they threaten them. If they say something they will lose their job." [164]

In February 1999, the San Francisco District office of the EEOC reached a $1,855,000 settlement with Tanimura & Antle, one of the largest lettuce growers and distributors in the United States. The EEOC alleged that a production manager for the company subjected employee Blanca Alfaro to quid pro quo sexual harassment, requiring "sexual favors" as a condition for employment. Alfaro also allegedly was subjected to a hostile work environment in the form of "constant unwelcome sexual advances by that production manager and another management employee." [165] Alfaro was fired shortly after she complained about the harassment. In addition, the EEOC alleged that Tanimura & Antle unlawfully retaliated against employee Elias Aragón after he protested the harassment and mistreatment of Blanca Alfaro. [166]

Sharing in the settlement will be an as-yet unknown number of current and former employees who were also subjected to sexual harassment in Salinas, California, Huron, California, and Yuma, Arizona. [167]

The EEOC's San Francisco office also settled a sexual harassment case in early 1999 against farm labor contractor C & M Packing, doing business as "Fresh West." [168] That case settled on behalf of four female claimants for $90,000. Like Tanimura & Antle, Fresh West has facilities in Yuma, Salinas, and Huron.

---

[164] Human Rights Watch interview, Yuma, Arizona, September 30, 1998.

[165] EEOC News (press release), "EEOC and Tanimura & Antle settle sexual harassment case in the agricultural industry," February 23, 1999, p. 1.

[166] Ibid. The retaliation against Mr. Aragón allegedly included verbal abuse, suspension without cause, and discharge.

[167] Human Rights Watch telephone interviews with EEOC attorney Cindy O'Hara, May 5, 1999, and April 25, 2000.

[168] Ibid.

These victories are attributable to EEOC outreach efforts and to the fact that, in the words of attorney O'Hara, "there are some brave women out there." Still, these two cases represent but a tiny fraction of the sexual harassment that is occurring in the fields and packing plants of the United States. The EEOC and state attorneys general—who also typically have civil rights jurisdiction—must make it a priority to engage in persistent outreach and education of workers, supervisors, farm labor contractors, and employers, and mount vigorous enforcement actions against harassers when complainants do come forward.

IV. U.S. LAWS AND THEIR ENFORCEMENT:
AN ONGOING FAILURE TO PROTECT CHILDREN
WORKING IN AGRICULTURE

Everyone violates the law one way or another.[169]

This report details the ways in which juvenile farmworkers are endangered and exploited on a daily basis. They work too many hours at too-young ages, burdened with fatigue when they should be studying, playing, or at school. They are not paid minimum wage. Their safety is compromised and their health is at risk. They are also, for the most part, unprotected by the U.S. government.

The United States prides itself on respect for human rights and frequently decries child labor practices in other countries. The Fair Labor Standards Act prohibits "oppressive child labor," defined as work that may be detrimental to children's health or well-being.[170] Yet hundreds of thousands of juveniles working in agriculture do labor under oppressive conditions in the U.S.

There are several reasons for this, high among them the fact that U.S. law is grossly and unjustifiably inadequate—not only does it offer insufficient protection for farmworker children and adolescents, but it offers them vastly less protection than it does for juveniles working in other occupations. Further worsening the situation, government enforcement of even these deficient laws is sporadic and weak. In addition, Congress has eviscerated in recent years the ability of publicly-funded legal aid offices to assist farmworkers, by prohibiting class-action lawsuits and prohibiting the representation of persons in the U.S. without proper documentation.[171] In sum, juvenile farmworkers are left with limited protection and few means of recourse when their rights are violated.

---

[169] Frank Zamudio, Arizona Department of Agriculture Industrial Hygienist, during a Human Rights Watch interview, October 1, 1998, in reference to agricultural employers.

[170] 29 U.S.C. section 203(l).

[171] These prohibitions apply to all legal aid offices receiving federal Legal Services Corporation funding. There is no private right of action for child labor violations. Prior to these restrictions (1996 for the ban on class-actions), however, legal aid offices could mount class action lawsuits regarding wage and hour violations.

The Fair Labor Standards Act and Enforcement by the Department of Labor

The Fair Labor Standards Act (FLSA) is the federal law that sets minimum ages for work, maximum numbers of work-hours per day and per week, and the minimum hourly wage. It originated in 1938 and has been modified numerous times since. Farmworkers originally were not protected at all by the law, and still are not covered fully. It was not until 1974 that restrictions on child labor in agriculture—albeit minimal—were incorporated.

The most glaring deficiency of the FLSA is its disparate treatment of farmworker and nonfarmworker children. Children working in nonagricultural occupations receive much greater protection against excessive hours of work, work at early ages, and work under hazardous conditions. In other words, as put by the General Accounting Office, "children can legally work in agriculture under conditions that would be illegal in other work settings."[172] For example:

- In agriculture, employers may hire children younger than twelve to work *unlimited hours* outside of school, provided the work takes place on a small farm with written parental consent. Outside of agriculture, the employment of children younger than twelve is prohibited.[173]

- In agriculture, employers may hire children aged twelve and thirteen to work *unlimited hours* outside of school, provided they have written parental consent or work on a farm where a parent is employed. Outside of agriculture, employment of children aged twelve and thirteen is forbidden.

- In agriculture, employers may hire children aged fourteen and fifteen to work *unlimited hours* outside of school. There is no parental consent requirement. Outside of agriculture, children aged fourteen and fifteen may work limited hours: up to forty hours in a nonschool week; up to eighteen hours in a school week; up to eight hours on a nonschool day; and up to three hours on a school day. In addition, outside of agriculture, fourteen and fifteen-year olds may not work before 7:00

---

[172] U.S. General Accounting Office, "Child Labor in Agriculture: Characteristics and Legality of Work," Washington, DC: U.S. General Accounting Office, 1998; GAO/HEHS-98-112R, p. 2.

[173] The FLSA allows for very limited exceptions to this, including work delivering newspapers, acting, and making evergreen wreaths.

a.m. or after 7:00 p.m. (9 p.m. in the summer). There are no similar restrictions protecting children working in agriculture.

- In agriculture, employers may require or allow sixteen and seventeen-year olds to work in hazardous occupations. In nonagricultural occupations, the minimum age for hazardous work is eighteen. This disparate treatment is particularly troublesome given agriculture's position as the most dangerous occupation for working children in the United States.[174]

Historically, agricultural employment practices in the U.S. have been regulated less than other occupations. Partly this is due to the United States inception as an agrarian society, and a lingering idealization of the agrarian life.[175] Partly it is due to the unique nature of farm work and the cycles of harvest, whose rapidly changing and sometimes unpredictable needs rarely coincide with a forty-hour per week, year-round work schedule.

For juvenile farmworkers, the differential treatment still present at the beginning of the 21st century stems from the vastly different circumstances found in the United States one hundred or even fifty years ago. In 1900, less than 10 percent of eighteen-year-olds finished high school,[176] and approximately 42 percent of the United States population lived on family farms.[177] Children of farm families were expected to work and learn all aspects of farming, which would continue to be their occupation into adulthood.

In 1938, when the FLSA was enacted, nearly a quarter of the United States population still lived on farms,[178] and only 50 percent of teenagers were finishing high school.[179] At that time, the FLSA included restrictions on nonagricultural work for children, but no restrictions whatsoever on farm work for children.

---

[174] Agriculture is the second most dangerous occupation after mining. Mine workers, however, must be at least eighteen years old.

[175] National Research Council, *Protecting Youth at Work*, pp. 146-148.

[176] Ibid., p. 21.

[177] Ibid., p. 142.

[178] Ibid., p. 147.

[179] Ibid., p. 21.

Today, only about 1.5 percent of United States residents live on farms.[180] Farms have changed form dramatically in the past decades; mechanization, specialization, fertilizers, and other technical innovations have led to the phenomenal growth of large-scale agriculture and the simultaneous decline of the small family farm. As a result, where once most children in agriculture were working on their own family farms, now most are working as hired hands for commercial enterprises.

Concurrent with this change in farming has been a change in education practices, including a heightened emphasis on secondary-school education for all. By 1997, the high school completion rate had risen to nearly 90 percent.[181] There exists now a widespread recognition that children not only have a *right* to a full education, but that they have a *need* for that education, and, without it, are likely to end up relegated to a minimum subsistence-level job (of which farm work is one example).

With all of these changes, the rationale for protecting child workers in agriculture less than all other child workers has evaporated. Children working on farms have the same need for sleep, health, education, and recreation as their nonfarmworking peers. Poverty does not change that, nor does it eliminate these children's right to enjoy full government protection. If excessive child labor is bad for some, then it is bad for all.

Occasionally, efforts to protect child workers from the deleterious effects of long hours in difficult and demanding jobs are met with skepticism and disapproval, on the grounds that limiting children's work hours will have a negative economic impact on them and their family. This is a short-sighted objection. Limiting the extreme aspects of child labor may reduce children's— and therefore families'—incomes in the short term. In the long-term, however, favoring education over menial labor vastly increases the probability that the cycle of poverty will be broken. One farmworker advocate in New York state observed that, "At a family level, parents usually want their kids to be able to work. Because the families are so caught up in their daily economic needs, it's difficult for them to look at the long-term effects on their kids of this dangerous, hazardous work."[182]

The disparate legal treatment outlined above is unfair and discriminatory. Furthermore, its impact is felt predominantly by juveniles of racial minorities.

---

[180] Ibid., p. 147, citing United States Bureau of the Census.

[181] Digest of Education Statistics, 1998 (http://nces.ed.gov/pubs99/digest98/chapter2.html).

[182] Human Rights Watch telephone interview with Dan Werner, Farmworker Legal Services of New York staff attorney, March 17, 2000.

This is due to the close correlation between race and occupation in farmwork. Nationally, approximately 85 percent of farmworkers, including juvenile farmworkers, are members of racial minorities; most of them are Latino.[183] In some regions, including Arizona and California, 99 percent of farmworkers are Latino. This means that the FLSA's two-tiered scheme of protection—one for farmworker children, one for all other working children—corresponds closely to race and ethnicity. By explicitly discriminating against farmworker children, most of whom are Latino, the law also engages in de facto discrimination along racial lines. This may violate international law, as will be discussed in the following chapter.

Proposed Amendments to the FLSA Regarding Child Labor in Agriculture

In the House of Representatives, Representative Tom Lantos (Democrat from California) has for the past twelve years introduced the "Young American Workers' Bill of Rights."[184] The bill is widely supported by children's advocates. It would enhance protection for many working children, including children working in agriculture. Among other provisions, the bill would amend the FLSA to:

- Specify that "oppressive child labor," forbidden under the Act, expressly applies to the employment of migrant farmworkers aged thirteen and under.

- For all working youth, restrict after-school work to fifteen to twenty hours per week, depending on age, and eliminate entirely before-school work.

- Broaden the FLSA's coverage to include all employers engaged in interstate commerce, regardless of their annual volume of sales.[185]

---

[183] National Center for Farmworker Health, "Who are America's Farmworkers?" http://www.ncfh.org/aboutfws/aboutfws.htm, accessed March 22, 1999, p. 2. The U.S. Bureau of Labor Statistics reported in 1998 that 44.9 percent of farm laborers are Latino. http://stats.bls.gov/pdf/cpsaatll.pdf. Based on our extensive research and consultation with national experts, Human Rights Watch considers this a gross underestimation.

[184] H.R.2119. As of November 1999, the bill is still in the House Committee on Education and the Workforce, Subcommittee on Workforce Protections.

[185] The federal government's authority to regulate commerce is rooted in Article I, Section 8 of the United States Constitution, which reads in its relevant part that "The

(Currently, the FLSA only applies to enterprises with $500,000 in annual sales or business.)

- Establish tougher criminal and civil penalties for child labor violations.

- Provide for closer coordination among federal and state child labor enforcement agencies.

In the 106th session of Congress, the proposed Young American Workers' Bill of Rights had fifty-eight cosponsors but enjoyed only limited bipartisan support.[186] It is not expected to pass. "Kids don't have high-priced lobbyists," Lantos aide Chris Walker told Human Rights Watch. "[The employers] have strong lobbyists."[187]

In past sessions, Senator Tom Harkin (Democrat from Iowa) has introduced Senate legislation titled "The Children's Act for Responsible Employment," or CARE. CARE, which was not introduced in the 106th session but will likely be introduced again in the future, seeks to amend the FLSA to: raise the age at which youth may engage in hazardous agricultural labor from sixteen to eighteen; apply the same age and hour restrictions to agricultural employment as to other forms of employment; and increase civil and criminal penalties for child labor violations.

Enforcement of the FLSA

It is estimated that there are at least one million child labor violations in the United States each year in agriculture and 100,000 minors working illegally— that is, in violation of child labor laws--on farms.[188] Only a tiny fraction of these violations are uncovered by the Wage and Hour Division (WHD) of the Department of Labor (DOL), which bears responsibility for the FLSA enforcement. In 1998, for example, WHD found 104 minors illegally employed

---

Congress shall have Power . . . [t]o regulate Commerce . . . among the several States." Accordingly, this authority is restricted to interstate commerce.

[186] Of the bill's fifty-eight cosponsors, only two—Tom Campbell (Republican from California) and John Porter (Republican from -Illinois)—are Republicans.

[187] Human Rights Watch telephone interview, March 2, 1999.

[188] United States General Accounting Office, "Hired Farmworkers: Health and Well-Being at Risk," Washington, D.C.: U.S. General Accounting Office, 1992; GAO/HRD-092-46, p. 22, citing an estimate by the National Child Labor Committee.

in agriculture[189]—one for every 1,000 estimated to be working illegally in the fields.

Inadequate Resources

Part of the problem is insufficient resources. The Wage and Hour Division does not have enough staff and funding to uncover and investigate the FLSA violations affecting minors in agriculture. As of late 1999, WHD had about 940 investigators to cover the entire country, inspecting and citing for violations against adult and child workers alike in all occupations, not just agriculture.[190] This is slightly *fewer* investigators than the agency had in 1987.[191] It works out to roughly one investigator for every 150,000 civilian workers.[192] Investigators are responsible for enforcing several dozens of laws.

None of these investigators, also called enforcement officers, are dedicated exclusively to child labor; only twenty-three are designated as farm labor specialists.[193]

Inadequate funding means that even this relatively small staff is underutilized. Child labor in agriculture currently is a "targeted initiative" for WHD, which means that the agency proactively enforces the law rather than waiting for complaints to arise before initiating investigations. "We have a very intense and vigorous enforcement program relating to agriculture," WHD's Child Labor Coordinator told Human Rights Watch.[194]

The money to carry out this program, however, appears lacking, forcing some investigators to cut short their efforts. In Arizona, a WHD investigator

---

[189] U.S. Department of Labor, "Compliance Highlights: 1998 Agricultural Activity Report, Wage and Hour Division," March 1999, p. 2.

[190] Human Rights Watch telephone interview with Corlis Sellers, WHD National Child Labor Coordinator, September 22, 1999.

[191] According to the GAO, there were 950 WHD enforcement officers in 1987. U.S. General Accounting Office, "Child Labor in Agriculture: Characteristics and Legality of Work," Washington, D.C.: U.S. General Accounting Office, 1998; GAO/HEHS-98-112R, p. 15.

[192] According to the Bureau of Labor Statistics, as of October 1999 there were 139,662,000 workers in the United States civilian labor force. Bureau of Labor Statistics, http://stats.bls.gov:80/eag.table.html.

[193] Human Rights Watch telephone interview with Corlis Sellers, WHD National Child Labor Coordinator, September 22, 1999.

[194] Human Rights Watch telephone interview with Corlis Sellers, WHD National Child Labor Coordinator, September 22, 1999.

had to call off a series of field investigations in the Willcox area after only two weeks, several weeks earlier than planned.[195] She was told there was a sudden budget crisis and that there were no more funds for travel. Given that Arizona's major agricultural areas are two to four hours from Phoenix, being grounded to headquarters drastically reduces enforcement possibilities. "There's not even enough money to go to Yuma," she lamented.[196] The Yuma area has about 75 percent of Arizona's farmworkers.

There is no doubt that widespread violations are out there and that WHD is capable of finding them when staff and resources are sufficiently allocated. In a 1998 investigation of grape growers, WHD found that, in California, more than 50 percent of farm labor contractors were violating the FLSA's minimum wage requirement.[197] In Arizona, 50 percent of grape growers and 60 percent of farm labor contractors were found in violation of the FLSA, and 53 percent of all grape field workers were owed back wages.[198] (The reports did not distinguish between juvenile and adult workers.) The problem is not an inability to find labor violations, but getting enough investigators out into the fields.

Child Labor in Agriculture Not a Priority

Until fiscal year 1998, WHD enforcement in agriculture was minimal. In fiscal year 1997, for example, the agency reported only fourteen child labor violations in agriculture.[199] "Until the Salad Bowl initiative, the Department of Labor's history was not to focus on agriculture at all," according to Darlene Adkins of the National Consumers League Child Labor Coalition. "Their levels of enforcement in agriculture were very low; basically they had no presence in agriculture."[200]

---

[195] Human Rights Watch telephone interview with Esther La Plante, WHD Farm Labor Specialist based in Phoenix, AZ, November 12, 1998.

[196] Ibid.

[197] U.S. Department of Labor, "Compliance Highlights: 1998 Agricultural Activity Report, Wage and Hour Division," March 1999, p. 2.

[198] U.S. Department of Labor Wage and Hour Division, Phoenix District Memorandum: "Phoenix District Grape Survey," November 10, 1998.

[199] U.S. General Accounting Office, "Child Labor in Agriculture: Characteristics and Legality of Work," Washington, D.C.: U.S. General Accounting Office, 1998; GAO/HEHS-98-112R, p. 12.

[200] Human Rights Watch telephone interview with Darlene Adkins, Coordinator, National Consumers League Child Labor Coalition, January 25, 1999.

The low priority of child labor in agriculture changed somewhat in fiscal year 1998 (October 1997 through September 1998), when the Department of Labor launched a "salad bowl" initiative. The "salad bowl" program targeted five crops—lettuce, tomatoes, cucumbers, onions, and garlic—for increased compliance within a five-year period. Labor law violations are common in all of these labor-intensive, hand-harvested crops. Different regional offices tailored their salad bowls to reflect area crops: in Arizona, chili peppers and green peppers were added; in New Jersey, blueberries; in Maryland, melons; in Louisiana, strawberries. The number of violations found increased considerably—from fourteen in 1997 to 104 in 1998—but still remained extraordinarily low.[201]

Ineffective Sanctions

Even when violations are found, sanctions generally are weak and ineffective. The Wage and Hour Division can assess civil money penalties in the case of child labor violations (for example, underage workers) and for repeated and willful wage violations (WHD does not have statutory authority to assess penalties for first-time wage violations). The amount of civil money penalties ordered for child labor violations in 1990 averaged only $212 per violation.[202] Wage and Hour Division officials told Human Rights Watch they did not know what the average penalty per child labor violation was in fiscal year 1998, but that the average penalty for all Wage and Hour violations was $971. [203] Since 1991, the maximum civil money penalty available for a nonwillful child labor violation has been $10,000. In practice, fines at that level are assessed only in cases of death or serious injury.[204]

For most growers, fines are relatively insignificant and it is easier and cheaper for them to violate the law and risk a fine than to comply with the law—especially since low rates of enforcement mean detection is rare. An

---

[201] By way of comparison, consider the Department of Labor statistical summaries for child labor violations uncovered in fiscal years 1989 through 1992: 1989: 24,074 in nonagricultural work; 299 in agriculture; 1990: 43,785 in nonagricultural work, 795 in agriculture; 1991: 28,390 in nonagricultural work, 334 in agriculture; 1992: 21,224 in nonagricultural work, 163 in agriculture.

[202] United States General Accounting Office, "Hired Farmworkers: Health and Well-Being at Risk," Washington, D.C.: U.S. General Accounting Office, 1992; GAO/HRD-092-46, p. 22.

[203] Human Rights Watch telephone interview with Corlis Sellers, WHD National Child Labor Coordinator, September 22, 1999.

[204] Ibid.

Arizona investigator told Human Rights Watch that "the fines are not strong enough. I had a grower say to me, "The fine is only $1,000; I'll just pay it and keep doing things as I am."[205]

The same investigator noted that the Phoenix district office, in a search for something more effective than civil money penalties, has increasingly turned to civil court injunctions, memoranda of understanding, and the FLSA's "hot goods" provision.[206] This trend, true of WHD's efforts nationwide, is a laudable and promising tactic.

The "hot goods" provision did not come into use by WHD until 1998, although it has been part of the FLSA since its origination in 1938. The provision prohibits the shipment in interstate commerce of any goods produced in violation of minimum wage, overtime, or child labor requirements.[207] It can be extremely effective, particularly in agriculture, in that it allows the WHD to seek temporary restraining orders preventing the movement of tainted goods. This creates great incentives for companies, growers, and other affected businesses to cooperate with WHD. Such cooperation has included future compliance agreements and arrangements for ongoing monitoring.

Use of the "hot goods" provision is still an exception rather than the rule. According to Department of Labor officials, statistics on its use are unavailable.[208]

Growers' Avoidance of Liability

In addition to weak sanctions, another common obstacle to the FLSA enforcement in agriculture is growers' distancing of themselves from their workers through the use of farm labor contractors. The maneuver, largely successful so far, seeks to avoid grower liability for labor violations by maintaining that the workers are not employees of the grower, but of the farm labor contractor exclusively. Of course, this is a total fiction. The growers own or lease the land and determine planting, cultivation, and harvesting methods

---

[205] Human Rights Watch telephone interview with Esther La Plante, WHD Farm Labor Specialist, November 17, 1999.

[206] Ibid.

[207] The provision as it pertains to child labor reads in part: "No producer, manufacturer, or dealer shall ship or deliver for shipment in commerce any goods produced in an establishment situated in the United States in or about which within thirty days prior to the removal of such goods therefrom any oppressive child labor has been employed." 29 U.S.C. section 212(a).

[208] Human Rights Watch telephone interview with Corlis Sellers, WHD National Child Labor Coordinator, September 22, 1999.

and schedules. They also pay, via the contractors, for all of the work that is done.

When growers avoid liability in this manner, there are two results. First, the growers escape accountability and are free to continue the violating practices; and second, workers' back pay, fines, and other penalties are unlikely to be collected, as many farm labor contractors are itinerant and without assets. In other words, nobody pays.

The Wage and Hour Division can beat this unjust maneuvering by finding joint employment—and therefore joint liability—between the grower and the farm labor contractor. WHD—which only recently began to seek joint liability in the farmworker context—determines joint employment by looking at a variety of factors, including: whether the grower has the authority to control, either directly or indirectly, the workers or the work they perform; whether the grower has control over employment conditions or wage payment; and whether the work performed is an integral part of the grower's business.[209]

Other labor experts contend that joint employment under the FLSA (as well as under the Migrant and Seasonal Agricultural Worker Protection Act (MSPA), also enforced by WHD[210]) is much broader, and includes all instances where growers "suffer or permit" the workers to work.[211] This approach more accurately reflects the language and intent of the FLSA, which defines "employ" as "to suffer or permit to work."[212]

Failure to Coordinate with States

Not all states regulate child labor in agriculture. Of those that do, not all enforce their laws. In a 1999 survey by the Child Labor Coalition, only ten states reported targeting child labor compliance in agriculture the previous

---

[209] U.S. Department of Labor Program Highlights, "Joint Employment and Independent Contractors Under the Migrant and Seasonal Agricultural Worker Protection Act," Fact Sheet ESA no. 97-31, pp. 2-3.

[210] The Migrant and Seasonal Agricultural Worker Protection Act (MSPA) requires agricultural employers to inform workers in writing of the terms of their employment, post information about worker rights, pay all wages owed when due and provide an itemized statement, and make and keep payroll records. 29 U.S.C. section 1801-1872.

[211] See, for example, Goldstein, Linder, Norton, and Ruckelshaus, "Enforcing Fair Labor Standards in the Modern American Sweatshop: Rediscovering the Statutory Definition of Employment," *UCLA Law Review* 46 (1999): 983.

[212] 29 U.S.C. section 203(g).

year.[213]   Of these ten states, only four—California, Florida, New Jersey, and
New York—reported a significant number of investigations.[214]

Inexplicably, the Wage and Hour Division does not coordinate its efforts
with those of the individual states.   A state's level of child labor law
enforcement is not taken into account in determining federal enforcement
efforts.[215]   Indeed, WHD does not even collect state enforcement statistics,
meaning they do not know which states, and to what extent, are participating at
all in combating child labor in agriculture.[216]

The Wage and Hour Division's failure to coordinate with the states—or at
least take into account state practices when formulating their own goals and
strategies—means that resources may not be used to their best advantage.
Efforts may be duplicated in some states; in others, a need for a heightened
WHD presence may go unnoticed.   In all cases, information sharing between
state and federal labor departments would be appropriate, useful, and likely to
increase positive enforcement results.

The Worker Protection Standard and other Environmental Protection Agency Regulations and their Enforcement

In 1992, the Environmental Protection Agency (EPA) promulgated a
Worker Protection Standard intended to "reduce the risks of illness or injury
resulting from . . . occupational exposures to pesticides . . ."[217] This regulation
was a significant step forward in protecting the health of farmworkers.   The
Worker Protection Standard forbids employers from requiring or allowing
workers, other than trained pesticide handlers, to enter or remain in areas being
treated with pesticides. It requires employers to notify workers when areas have
been treated by pesticides, either orally, by means of prominently-posted
"Danger" signs, or both, depending on the pesticide's labeling statement.   The
Standard further requires that workers be trained regarding pesticide safety,
pesticide-related illnesses, and emergency responses to pesticide exposure.

---

[213] Child Labor Coalition, "1999 Child Labor State Survey," National Consumers
League, Washington, D.C., 1999, pp. 6-7.

[214] Ibid.

[215] Human Rights Watch telephone interview with Corlis Sellers, WHD National
Child Labor Coordinator, September 22, 1999.

[216] Ibid.

[217] 40 C.F.R. (Code of Federal Regulations) section 170.1. See 40 C.F.R. section
170 and following sections for the entire Worker Protection Standard.

Restricted-entry intervals (REIs) are also set by the EPA but do not form part of the Worker Protection Standard itself.[218] Restricted-entry intervals refer to the period of time after a pesticide's application during which workers should not be in the treated areas. Generally speaking, the shortest REI is twelve hours and the longest is seventy-two hours.[219] Dry conditions—as in the Arizona desert—may necessitate a longer REI, particularly among toxicity category I pesticides, which are the most toxic.[220]

The problem with the Worker Protection Standard and the REI regulations is that they are formulated with adults—and only adults—in mind. Restricted-entry intervals are determined using the model of a 154-pound adult male. There is no prohibition on children mixing, handling, or applying pesticides. Despite the greater vulnerability of juveniles to pesticides, there is no special consideration for them in the EPA regulations at all.

The Worker Protection Standard, although a federal regulation, is enforced by the individual states, usually by their departments of agriculture.[221] In an interview with Human Rights Watch, a top EPA official said that the agency "has concern for the lack of consistency state to state regarding enforcement. . . . We're talking about enforcement of a national standard, and we'd like to think there was [consistency in enforcement], but we're not that naive."[222] A national assessment by EPA of how the states are implementing and enforcing the regulations is underway as of the end of 1999.[223]

In response to outside concern and inquiries—notably by the General Accounting Office[224] and a coalition of prominent nongovernmental

---

[218] See "Restricted-entry statements," 40 C.F.R. section 156.208.

[219] 40 C.F.R. section 156.208(c)(2)(i)-(iii).

[220] Ibid., section 156.208(c)(2)(i).

[221] Human Rights Watch telephone interview with Kevin Keaney, EPA Branch Chief for Certification and Worker Protection, October 19, 1999. According to Keaney, in a few states it is the state public health or environmental agency that enforces the EPA regulations, rather than the department of agriculture. It is up to the individual state to decide its enforcement strategy.

[222] Ibid.

[223] Ibid.

[224] Representative Henry Waxman commissioned a study by the GAO of the protection of children in agriculture. Preliminary results of the inquiry are found in: U.S. General Accounting Office, "Child Labor in Agriculture: Characteristics and Legality of Work," Washington, DC: U.S. General Accounting Office, 1998; GAO/HEHS-98-112R. The GAO's final report is due in early 2000.

organizations[225]—the EPA also began in the late 1990s to look at children as a special population in need of protection. As of this writing in late 1999, however, no new protections for farmworker juveniles had been proposed by the EPA.

Arizona Enforcement of EPA Regulations

In Arizona, pesticide enforcement is carried out by the Environmental Services Division of the Arizona Department of Agriculture. In addition to pesticide compliance and enforcement, the division is responsible for registering and licensing feed, fertilizers, and pesticides.

There are two immediate areas of concern regarding Arizona's enforcement of federal pesticide regulations. The first, probably true for all state agriculture departments, is that the department itself and most of its inspectors have traditionally served the needs of growers, not workers. This is reflected in the Department of Agriculture's Mission Statement: "To regulate and support Arizona agriculture in a manner that encourages farming, ranching, and agribusiness while protecting consumers and natural resources."[226] It contains not a word about protecting agricultural workers.

This attitude was revealed also in an informal and unsolicited comment made to Human Rights Watch by an inspector in Yuma, who said that when growers violated worker safety standards he preferred not to cite them. "I prefer to work *with* the grower," he said. "I prefer to get voluntary compliance."[227] A federal EPA official also acknowledged that state agriculture inspectors may be biased toward growers.[228]

A second problem is that only two of Arizona's eleven Environmental Services inspectors are bilingual in English and Spanish. Given that

---

[225] In May 1999, the following organizations sent a public letter to the EPA urging that pesticides be tested for their toxicity to children's developing nervous systems, and expressing their concern over an EPA decision to remove a Congressionally-mandated "10X" (meaning requiring a margin of safety for children ten times that required for adults) safety standard designed to protect children: Natural Resources Defense Council, Learning Disabilities Association of America, Consumers Union, Physicians for Social Responsibility, Science and Environmental Health Network, and the U.S. Public Interest Research Group.

[226] Arizona Department of Agriculture homepage, , updated November 22, 1999.

[227] Human Rights Watch was not interviewing this inspector and his name is not available. The comment was made on October 1, 1998.

[228] Human Rights Watch telephone interview with Kevin Keaney, EPA Branch Chief for Certification and Worker Protection, October 19, 1999.

approximately 99 percent of Arizona's farmworkers are Spanish-speaking,[229] the lack of bilingual inspectors raises serious doubts regarding the ability of Arizona to adequately ensure pesticide-use compliance and the commitment of the state to this mandate.

Field Sanitation Standards: Federal OSHA and OSHA-Approved State Plans and their Enforcement

In 1987, the federal Occupational Safety and Health Administration (OSHA) issued a Field Sanitation Standard. The Standard requires agricultural employers to provide workers with:

(1) Cool and potable drinking water in sufficient amounts, dispensed by single-use drinking cups or by fountains and readily accessible to all; and

(2) One toilet and a handwashing facility for each twenty employees, located within a quarter-mile walk.

OSHA predicted that implementation of this standard would reduce by hundreds of thousands the annual incidence of farmworker illnesses, injuries, and deaths, including heat-related deaths and injuries, parasitic intestinal illnesses, pesticide-related illnesses, and urinary tract infections.[230]

Aside from enforcement problems, the primary weakness of the Field Sanitation Standard is that Congress annually limits its application to agricultural establishments that employ eleven or more people as hand laborers.[231] Farms employing fewer than eleven hand laborers are exempt. As a result, hundreds of thousands of farmworkers, including juveniles, may not have access to basic sanitation and health requirements. Even worse, the limit of OSHA jurisdiction to farms with eleven or more workers is absolute, extending

---

[229] Estimate provided by Gary Restaino, former staff attorney with Community Legal Services Farmworker Program, in a telephone interview with Human Rights Watch, April 26, 1999.

[230] U.S. Department of Labor, Occupational Safety and Health Administration, "OSHA's Field Sanitation Standard," Fact Sheet No. OSHA 92-25, p. 2.

[231] As noted, Congress exempts small farms from enforcement of OSHA standards by attaching riders to annual appropriation bills; see, e.g., U.S. Departments of Labor, Health and Human Services, and Education, and Related Agencies Appropriations Act, 1998, HR 2264, 105th Congress. National Research Council, *Protecting Youth at Work*, p. 141.

far beyond field sanitation—it applies even to cases where workers face unsafe working conditions or where a catastrophe or fatality has occurred. Whatever happens on a farm with ten or fewer employees, OSHA may not investigate.

Individual states may develop and operate their own occupational safety and health programs. These programs, called State Plans, must be approved and monitored by federal OSHA. Once in place, they supplant (with limited exceptions) direct federal OSHA enforcement in that state.

As of December 1999, twenty-one states had approved State Plans.[232] Of these, only four—Alaska, Arizona, Oregon, and Washington—required farms with ten or fewer workers to comply with field sanitation standards.[233] Arizona's state-plan jurisdiction extends to all farms with five or more workers. Some employers attempt to dodge the sanitation regulations by splitting up their workers into crews of four, each in a different field (thereby giving the appearance of no more than four workers), or by hiring their labor via farm labor contractors.[234]

Even when the standards do apply, violations are rampant. According to the General Accounting Office, violations were found in 69 percent of all federal field inspections conducted in 1990.[235] Despite this high rate of violations, enforcement is minimal. The GAO reported in 1998 that "OSHA has devoted less than 3 percent of its inspections over the past 5 years to agriculture, even though agriculture is often considered to be one of the most hazardous industries."[236]

---

[232] The states are Alaska, Arizona, California, Hawai'i, Indiana, Iowa, Kentucky, Maryland, Michigan, Minnesota, Nevada, New Mexico, North Carolina, Oregon, South Carolina, Tennessee, Utah, Vermont, Virginia, Washington, and Wyoming. Puerto Rico and the Virgin Islands also have approved plans, and Connecticut and New York have plans that cover public sector employment only. U.S. Department of Labor, Occupational Safety and Health Administration, "State Occupational Safety and Health Plans," http://www.osha~slc.gov/.

[233] United States General Accounting Office, "Hired Farmworkers: Health and Well-Being at Risk," Washington, DC: U.S. General Accounting Office, 1992; GAO/HRD-092-46, p. 20.

[234] Human Rights Watch interview with Art Morelos, Arizona Industrial Commission Compliance Supervisor, Tucson, Arizona, October 15, 1998.

[235] United States General Accounting Office, "Hired Farmworkers: Health and Well-Being at Risk," Washington, DC: U.S. General Accounting Office, 1992; GAO/HRD-092-46, p. 20.

[236] United States General Accounting Office, "Child Labor in Agriculture: Characteristics and Legality of Work," Washington, D.C.: U.S. General Accounting Office, 1998; GAO/HEHS-98-112R, p. 15.

States with their own OSHA plans generally fare no better, and may have even lower rates of compliance, depending on their standards and the vigor with which inspections take place and violations are cited and fined. A 1990 study in North Carolina found that "only 4 percent of the hired farmworkers surveyed had access to drinking water, . . . handwashing and toilet facilities."[237]

Arizona OSHA

In Arizona, the state most closely examined by Human Rights Watch, there is very little enforcement of field sanitation standards or other health and safety regulations. The Industrial Commission's Division of Occupational Safety and Health (hereinafter Arizona OSHA) has jurisdiction over all farm health and safety issues, not just field sanitation. The agency, however, does not make *any* farm inspections on its own initiative. "We don't do farm inspections unless we receive a complaint from an employee or a referral from another government agency," said Art Morelos, Compliance Supervisor for the Tucson office.[238] Morelos noted that "I'm sure a lot [of farmworkers] get hurt that we never hear about."[239]

The Tucson office is responsible for seven southern Arizona counties, including Yuma County, where about 75 percent of Arizona farmwork takes place. The office averages only thirty to fifty farm inspections a year, almost all of them the result of referrals from farmworker advocates in other agencies, including legal aid workers.

There is general agreement that farmworkers rarely initiate complaints themselves. The primary reason, discussed earlier in this report, is fear of retribution. Farmworkers are simply too vulnerable; to complain is to risk their job. In addition to fear, farmworkers are unlikely to know that they have a right to clean and plentiful drinking water, toilet facilities, and a place to wash their hands. Morelos acknowledged both of these concerns. "They're afraid of losing their jobs; afraid to speak up because of retaliation. They don't know what their rights are."

---

[237] General Accounting Office, "Hired Farmworkers: Health and Well-Being at Risk," p. 20.., citing Maureen Sweeney and Stephen Ciesieski, *Where Work is Hazardous to Your Health* (Raleigh, North Carolina: Farmworkers Legal Services of North Carolina, Apr. 1990).

[238] Human Rights Watch interview, October 15, 1998.

[239] Ibid.

Nor are they likely to learn what their rights are, as Arizona's state OSHA does not engage in farmworker education regarding minimum sanitation standards. Even if workers did know that their rights were being violated and wanted to complain, however, they would have yet another hurdle to cross—filing the complaint. Both state regulations and state-OSHA policy requires all complaints, including complaints from workers, to be submitted in writing.[240] Nor is there a toll-free number that workers can call, whether to make a complaint, find out how to make a complaint, or ask for information. The vast majority of farmworkers, of course, live in rural areas, are very poor, and have minimal educational backgrounds. Many do not speak English. Given these conditions and circumstances, it is not surprising that worker complaints are rare.[241]

Several farmworker advocates reported that, when they do make referrals to state OSHA, the response is slow and ineffective. They also complained of a rigid insistence on receiving written information regarding violations, a requirement that the regulations themselves do not extend to referring agencies. One advocate said, "I call with a complaint, they tell me to fax it in. Fax it! I'm in the middle of nowhere! Do they think farmworkers are going to be able to fax in their complaints?"[242]

Arizona OSHA has shown little interest in establishing a presence outside of the two major metropolitan areas of Tucson and Phoenix. There is no office in Yuma, not even a seasonal office during the peak growing season. OSHA trips to remote areas—where much agricultural work takes place, and where, because of a lack of oversight and government intervention, abuses are most plentiful—are reportedly very rare.

Part of the problem appears to be due to understaffing. The Tucson office of Arizona OSHA, responsible for an area with approximately one million residents, has five inspectors. They have jurisdiction over all workplaces except mines and on federal installations and reservations. They are so understaffed

---

[240] "An employee . . . who believes that a violation of a safety or health standard or regulation exists that threatens physical harm or that an imminent danger exists may request an investigation by giving notice to the director or his authorized representative of such violation or danger. Any such notice shall be reduced to writing . . ." 23 Arizona Revised Statutes section 408(F)

[241] Compliance Supervisor Art Morelos estimated that 95 to 99 percent of all agriculture-related complaints are referrals from other agencies rather than direct complaints from workers. Human Rights Watch interview, September 20, 1999.

[242] Human Rights Watch interview, September 30, 1998. The advocate interviewed preferred to remain unnamed.

that they do not investigate farm accidents unless there is a fatality or a catastrophe (three or more people hospitalized due to a single accident).[243]

When occupational violations are found and agricultural employers cited, it is usually the farm labor contractor alone who faces liability. "The growers got wise," said Art Morelos. "Because whoever pays the workers has to also pay the workers comp insurance, transportation insurance, deal with sanitation, worry about OSHA, etc."[244] He also noted that farm labor contractors generally have fewer resources and are more difficult to collect fines from than are growers. Unlike the U.S. Department of Labor, Arizona OSHA is not yet pursuing the growers themselves via a theory of joint liability.

---

[243]   Human Rights Watch interview with Art Morelos, Arizona Industrial Commission Compliance Supervisor, Tucson, Arizona, October 15, 1998.

[244] Human Rights Watch interview with Art Morelos, September 20, 1999.

V. FAILURE TO COMPLY WITH INTERNATIONAL LAW

The United States violates multiple provisions of international treaties in its treatment of farmworker children. The failure to protect farmworker children equally with nonfarmworker children violates the right to equal protection of the law, found not only in the United States Constitution but also in the International Covenant on Civil and Political Rights and the Convention on the Rights of the Child. The United States also is in violation of provisions requiring the protection of children from economic exploitation and from dangerous or otherwise harmful working conditions.

Additional international standards are violated by the failure of the U.S. to enforce its laws that *do* purport to protect children working in agriculture. These various infractions of international law are discussed below.

Violation of International Non-Discrimination Laws

United States law—which sets a lower standard of protection for child farmworkers than for children working in other occupations—violates various international treaties forbidding discriminatory laws and practices. Article 26 of the International Covenant on Civil and Political Rights (ICCPR) states that "[a]ll persons are equal before the law and are entitled without any discrimination to the equal protection of the law. . . ." The United States has been a State Party to the ICCPR since 1992. Article 2 of the Convention on the Rights of the Child requires States Parties (which the U.S. is not, having signed but not ratified the Convention) to respect and ensure all rights enumerated in the convention—which include several applicable to child farmworkers (see below)—without discrimination of any kind. Among those bases of discrimination explicitly forbidden are race, color, language, and national, ethnic or social origin.

ILO Convention Concerning the Prohibition and Immediate Elimination of the Worst Forms of Child Labour (Worst Forms of Child Labor Convention)

In 1999, the International Labour Organization adopted a convention calling for all ratifying Member States "to secure the prohibition and elimination of the worst forms of child labour as a matter of urgency."[245] The United States ratified this convention on December 2, 1999. Prior to adoption of the convention, the United States government spoke strongly in its favor, urging

---

[245] International Labour Organization Convention Concerning the Prohibition and Immediate Action for the Elimination of the Worst Forms of Child Labour (Worst Forms of Child Labor Convention), Article 1.

ILO Members to "join together and to say there are some things we cannot and will not tolerate."[246]

Unfortunately, the United States itself witnesses and tolerates extreme forms of child labor that undoubtedly fall within the intended purview of the Worst Forms of Child Labour Convention.

Under the convention, "the worst forms of child labour" include, among others, "work which, by its nature or the circumstances in which it is carried out, is likely to harm the health, safety or morals of children."[247] Exactly what constitutes such types of work is left to be determined by Member States, in consultation with employer and worker organizations and in consideration of international standards, particularly the ILO Worst Forms of Child Labour Recommendation.[248] This Recommendation, adopted in 1999 in conjunction with the convention of the same name, states that:

> In determining the types of work referred to under Article 3(d) of the Convention [the "worst forms of child labour" definition], and in identifying where they exist, consideration should be given, as a minimum, to:
>
> (a) work which exposes children to physical, emotional or sexual abuse;
>
> (b) work underground, under water, at dangerous heights or in confined spaces;
>
> (c) work with dangerous machinery, equipment and tools, or which involves the manual handling or transport of heavy loads;
>
> (d) work in an unhealthy environment which may, for example, expose children to hazardous substances, agents or processes, or to temperatures, noise levels, or vibrations damaging to their health;

---

[246] Office of the Press Secretary, The White House, "Remarks by the President to the International Labor Organization Conference," June 16, 1999.

[247] Worst Forms of Child Labor Convention, Article 3(d).

[248] Ibid., Article 4.

(e) work under particularly difficult conditions such as work for long hours or during the night or work which does not allow for the possibility of returning home each day.[249]

As seen in this report, children working in agriculture in the United States—who number in the hundreds of thousands—face the risks outlined in subparagraphs (c) through (e): work with dangerous machinery, equipment, and tools; work in an unhealthy environment, including exposure to hazardous substances, notably pesticides; and work for long hours, during the night, or without the possibility of returning home each day. In addition, female farmworkers may face the danger of subparagraph (a) (exposure to sexual abuse).

It is apparent, then, that farm work in the U.S. sometimes runs a high risk of harming the health and safety of children, and does in many cases meet the definitional requirements of the "worst forms of child labor." Consequently, as a ratifying member state of the Worst Forms of Child Labour Convention, the United States is under an affirmative obligation to take immediate and effective steps to ascertain what forms and conditions of child labor in agriculture violate the convention and then eliminate them.

The convention further calls on member states to: prevent children from engaging in the worst forms of child labor; provide direct assistance for the removal of children already engaged in the worst forms of child labor; identify and reach out to children at risk; and take account of the special situation of girls.[250]

Far from acknowledging the danger of farm work to children and taking these appropriate steps, the United States *by law* permits children to engage in agricultural labor with fewer restrictions than children working in other areas. This includes permitting children to engage in hazardous agricultural work.

Even worse, the United States government mistakenly contends that the United States is already in full compliance with the Worst Forms of Child Labour Convention. While eager to point out abusive child labor practices in Guatemala, Brazil, Pakistan, and other developing countries,[251] the United States is myopic when it comes to domestic abuses. In announcing U.S. ratification of the Convention, the White House declared that ratification "would require no

---

[249] International Labour Organization Recommendation Concerning the Prohibition and Immediate Elimination of the Worst Forms of Child Labour, paragraph 3.

[250] Worst Forms of Child Labour Convention, Article 7.

[251] See, for example, Office of the Press Secretary, the White House, "Remarks by the President at Signing of ILO Convention 182," December 2, 1999.

changes in U.S. law and practice. U.S. law already prohibits the worst forms of child labor, and law enforcement and social service programs are in place to implement the requirements of the Convention."[252]

This conclusion was the work of "a Presidential advisory group of labor, business, and government experts."[253] This "advisory group" appears to fall substantially short of the broad-spectrum consultative process called for in article 4 of the Convention and mentioned above. The "advisory group" utilized is a standing advisory panel, the Tripartite Advisory Panel on International Labor Standards.[254] It consists of attorneys representing the following:

- the United States Secretary of Labor;
- the United States Secretary of State;
- the United States Secretary of Commerce;
- the President of the AFL-CIO (American Federation of Labor and Congress of Industrial Organizations);
- the President of the U.S. Council for International Business.[255]

Legal counsel for the Presidential Advisors on National Security and Economics also participate.[256]

In other words, the U.S. "advisory group," consisted of five people appointed from government, one from business, and one from labor—a lopsided arrangement at best.

In its report, this advisory panel concluded that there would be no need for the U.S. government to formally consult with worker and employer organizations to identify where the worst forms of child labor exist (as required by Article 4(2)) because "[e]mployer and worker organizations, along with the

---

[252] Office of the Press Secretary, the White House, "President Clinton Ratifies the New ILO Convention on the Worst Forms of Child Labor: Promoting Core Labor Standards Around the World," December 2, 1999.

[253] Ibid.

[254] Human Rights Watch telephone interview with Charlie Spring, Director for the Office of the International Labor Organization, Washington, D.C., February 1, 2000.

[255] Report of the Tripartite Advisory Panel on International Labor Standards to the President's Committee on the International Labor Organization Regarding Convention No. 182 on the Worst Forms of Child Labor, T.Doc. 106-005-S1P-99-3, p. 2.

[256] Human Rights Watch telephone interview with Charlie Spring, Director for the Office of the International Labor Organization, Washington, D.C., February 1, 2000.

general public, have regular access to the Department of Labor and other government agencies . . ."[257]

The Convention on the Rights of the Child

The United States has signed but not ratified the Convention on the Rights of the Child (CRC). (The only other country that has not ratified the convention is Somalia, which has no functioning government.) Notwithstanding the failure of the U.S. to ratify it, the convention provides strong guidance as to the *minimum* protections to which children—defined as all those under the age of eighteen—are entitled. Several provisions of the convention apply to farmworker children.

The United States' violation of article 32 is the most glaring of its violations and is implicated directly by the findings of this report. This article addresses exploitation in employment. It states that children have a right "to be protected from economic exploitation and from performing any work that is likely to be hazardous or to interfere with the child's education, or to be harmful to the child's health or physical, mental, spiritual, moral or social development." The article calls on governments to take appropriate legislative, administrative, social and educational measures in this regard, and especially to provide for a minimum age of employment, appropriate regulation of work hours and conditions of employment, and appropriate sanctions to ensure enforcement of the article.

Article 24 recognizes the right of all children to a high standard of health and to healthcare facilities, and calls on governments "to ensure the provision of necessary medical assistance and health care to all children." Compliance with this standard is compromised in the U.S. by the spotty availability of health care and medical clinics for farmworking children (as well as all children—farmworkers and otherwise—of agricultural laborers). Farmworkers don't usually earn enough to pay for health care out-of-pocket, and rarely can afford health insurance. According to a spokesperson for the National Center for Farmworker Health, almost all farmworker children are eligible for Medicaid,[258] but difficulties in enrollment and the lack of state-to-state portability, however,

---

[257] Report of the Tripartite Advisory Panel on International Labor Standards, p. 20. Article 4(2) of the Worst Forms of Child Labor Convention states that "The competent authority, after consultation with the organizations of employers and workers concerned, shall identify where the types of work so determined exist."

[258] Medicaid is a federally-subsidized health insurance program for low-income people.

mean that relatively few are able to utilize it.[259]   Less than 15 percent of farmworkers have access to federally-subsidized health clinics.[260]

Article 28 of the convention recognizes the right of all children to education. It instructs governments to make education "available and accessible to all," and to "[t]ake measures to encourage regular attendance at schools and the reduction of drop-out rates." In the United States, the school drop-out rate among farmworker children is 45 percent.

Finally, article 3 of the Convention on the Rights of the Child states that "In all actions concerning children . . . the best interests of the child shall be a primary consideration."

---

[259] Human Rights Watch telephone interview with Gina Rose Lombardi, Public Information Coordinator, National Center for Farmworker Health, March 22, 1999. States may take up to forty-five days to process Medicaid applications; a worker's eligibility must be re-validated every one to six months; and only some states reciprocate on Medicaid eligibility. National Advisory Council on Migrant Health, *Losing Ground: The Condition of Farmworkers in America* (Bethesda, MD: Department of Health and Human Services, 1995), pp. 8-9.

[260] National Advisory Council on Migrant Health, *Losing Ground: The Condition of Farmworkers in America* (Bethesda, MD: Department of Health and Human Services, 1995), p. 10.

APPENDIX A: SELECTED PROVISIONS OF THE FAIR LABOR STANDARDS ACT, 29 U.S.C. §§ 201 - 219

Sec. 206. Minimum wage

(a) Employees engaged in commerce; . . . agricultural employees

Every employer shall pay to each of his employees who in any workweek is engaged in commerce or in the production of goods for commerce, or is employed in an enterprise engaged in commerce or in the production of goods for commerce, wages at the following rates:

(1)   except as otherwise provided in this section, not less than $4.25 an hour during the period ending on September 30, 1996, not less than $4.75 an hour during the year beginning on October 1, 1996, and not less than $5.15 an hour beginning September 1, 1997 . . .

Sec. 207. Maximum hours

(a) Employees engaged in interstate commerce; additional applicability to employees pursuant to subsequent amendatory provisions

(1) Except as otherwise provided in this section, no employer shall employ any of his employees who in any workweek is engaged in commerce or in the production of goods for commerce, or is employed in an enterprise engaged in commerce or in the production of goods for commerce, for a workweek longer than forty hours unless such employee receives compensation for his employment in excess of the hours above specified at a rate not less than one and one-half times the regular rate at which he is employed.

(2) No employer shall employ any of his employees who in any workweek is engaged in commerce or in the production of goods for commerce, or is employed in an enterprise engaged in commerce or in the production of goods for commerce, and who in such workweek is brought within the purview of this subsection by the amendments made to this chapter by the Fair Labor Standards Amendments of 1966 –

(A) for a workweek longer than forty-four hours during the first year from the effective date of the Fair Labor Standards Amendments of 1966,

(B) for a workweek longer than forty-two hours during the second year from such date, or

(C) for a workweek longer than forty hours after the expiration of the second year from such date, unless such employee receives compensation for his employment in excess of the hours above specified at a rate not less than one and one-half times the regular rate at which he is employed.

Sec. 212. Child labor provisions

Restrictions on shipment of goods; prosecution; conviction

No producer, manufacturer, or dealer shall ship or deliver for shipment in commerce any goods produced in an establishment situated in the United States in or about which within thirty days prior to the removal of such goods therefrom any oppressive child labor has been employed: Provided, That any such shipment or delivery for shipment of such goods by a purchaser who acquired them in good faith in reliance on written assurance from the producer, manufacturer, or dealer that the goods were produced in compliance with the requirements of this section, and who acquired such goods for value without notice of any such violation, shall not be deemed prohibited by this subsection: And provided further, That a prosecution and conviction of a defendant for the shipment or delivery for shipment of any goods under the conditions herein prohibited shall be a bar to any further prosecution against the same defendant for shipments or deliveries for shipment of any such goods before the beginning of said prosecution.

(b) Investigations and inspections

The Secretary of Labor or any of his authorized representatives, shall make all investigations and inspections under section 211(a) of this title with respect to the employment of minors, and, subject to the direction and control of the Attorney General, shall bring all actions under section 217 of this title to enjoin any act or practice which is unlawful by reason of the existence of oppressive child labor, and shall administer all other provisions of this chapter relating to oppressive child labor.

(c) Oppressive child labor

No employer shall employ any oppressive child labor in commerce or in the production of goods for commerce or in any enterprise engaged in commerce or in the production of goods for commerce.

(d) Proof of age

In order to carry out the objectives of this section, the Secretary may by regulation require employers to obtain from any employee proof of age.

Sec. 213. Exemptions
(a) Minimum wage and maximum hour requirements

The provisions of sections 206 **[minimum wage]** (except subsection (d) in the case of paragraph (1) of this subsection) and section 207 **[maximum hours and overtime]** of this title shall not apply with respect to –

(6) any employee employed in agriculture (A) if such employee is employed by an employer who did not, during any calendar quarter during the preceding calendar year, use more than five hundred man-days of agricultural labor, (B) if such employee is the parent, spouse, child, or other member of his employer's immediate family, (C) if such employee (i) is employed as a hand harvest laborer and is paid on a piece rate basis in an operation which has been, and is customarily and generally recognized as having been, paid on a piece rate basis in the region of employment, (ii) commutes daily from his permanent residence to the farm on which he is so employed, and (iii) has been employed in agriculture less than thirteen weeks during the preceding calendar year, (D) if such employee (other than an employee described in clause (C) of this subsection) (i) is sixteen years of age or under and is employed as a hand harvest laborer, is paid on a piece rate basis in an operation which has been, and is customarily and generally recognized as having been, paid on a piece rate basis in the region of employment, (ii) is employed on the same farm as his parent or person standing in the place of his parent, and (iii) is paid at the same piece rate as employees over age sixteen are paid on the same farm, or (E) if such employee is principally engaged in the range production of livestock; or

(b) Maximum hour requirements
The provisions of section 207 of this title shall not apply with respect to –

(12) any employee employed in agriculture or in connection with the operation or maintenance of ditches, canals, reservoirs, or waterways, not owned or operated for profit, or operated on a sharecrop basis, and which are used exclusively for supply and storing of water, at least 90 percent of which was ultimately delivered for agricultural purposes during the preceding calendar year; or

(c) Child labor requirements
(1) Except as provided in paragraph (2) or (4), the provisions of section 212 of this title relating to child labor shall not apply to any employee employed in agriculture outside of school hours for the school district where such employee is living while he is so employed, if such employee -
(A) is less than twelve years of age and (i) is employed by his parent, or by a person standing in the place of his parent, on a farm owned or

operated by such parent or person, or (ii) is employed, with the consent of his parent or person standing in the place of his parent, on a farm, none of the employees of which are (because of subsection (a)(6)(A) of this section) required to be paid at the wage rate prescribed by section 206(a)(5) of this title,

(B) is twelve years or thirteen years of age and (i) such employment is with the consent of his parent or person standing in the place of his parent, or (ii) his parent or such person is employed on the same farm as such employee, or

(C) is fourteen years of age or older.

(2) The provisions of section 212 of this title relating to child labor shall apply to an employee below the age of sixteen employed in agriculture in an occupation that the Secretary of Labor finds and declares to be particularly hazardous for the employment of children below the age of sixteen, except where such employee is employed by his parent or by a person standing in the place of his parent on a farm owned or operated by such parent or person.

(3) The provisions of section 212 of this title relating to child labor shall not apply to any child employed as an actor or performer in motion pictures or theatrical productions, or in radio or television productions.

(4)

(A) An employer or group of employers may apply to the Secretary for a waiver of the application of section 212 of this title to the employment for not more than eight weeks in any calendar year of individuals who are less than twelve years of age, but not less than ten years of age, as hand harvest laborers in an agricultural operation which has been, and is customarily and generally recognized as being, paid on a piece rate basis in the region in which such individuals would be employed. The Secretary may not grant such a waiver unless he finds, based on objective data submitted by the applicant, that -

(i) the crop to be harvested is one with a particularly short harvesting season and the application of section 212 of this title would cause severe economic disruption in the industry of the employer or group of employers applying for the waiver;

(ii) the employment of the individuals to whom the waiver would apply would not be deleterious to their health or well-being;

(iii) the level and type of pesticides and other chemicals used would not have an adverse effect on the health or well-being of the individuals to whom the waiver would apply;

(iv) individuals age twelve and above are not available for such employment; and

(v) the industry of such employer or group of employers has traditionally and substantially employed individuals under twelve years of age without displacing substantial job opportunities for individuals over sixteen years of age.

(B) Any waiver granted by the Secretary under subparagraph (A) shall require that -

(i) the individuals employed under such waiver be employed outside of school hours for the school district where they are living while so employed;

(ii) such individuals while so employed commute daily from their permanent residence to the farm on which they are so employed; and

(iii) such individuals be employed under such waiver (I) for not more than eight weeks between June 1 and October 15 of any calendar year, and (II) in accordance with such other terms and conditions as the Secretary shall prescribe for such individuals' protection.

(5)

(A) In the administration and enforcement of the child labor provisions of this chapter, employees who are 16 and 17 years of age shall be permitted to load materials into, but not operate or unload materials from, scrap paper balers and paper box compactors -

(i) that are safe for 16- and 17-year-old employees loading the scrap paper balers or paper box compactors; and

(ii) that cannot be operated while being loaded.

(B) For purposes of subparagraph (A), scrap paper balers and paper box compactors shall be considered safe for 16- or 17-year-old employees to load only if -

(i)

(I) the scrap paper balers and paper box compactors meet the American National Standards Institute's Standard ANSI Z245.5 1990 for scrap paper balers and Standard ANSI Z245.2-1992 for paper box compactors; or

(II) the scrap paper balers and paper box compactors meet an applicable standard that is adopted by the American National

Standards Institute after August 6, 1996, and that is certified by the Secretary to be at least as protective of the safety of minors as the standard described in subclause (I);

(ii) the scrap paper balers and paper box compactors include an on-off switch incorporating a key-lock or other system and the control of the system is maintained in the custody of employees who are 18 years of age or older;

(iii) the on-off switch of the scrap paper balers and paper box compactors is maintained in an off position when the scrap paper balers and paper box compactors are not in operation; and

(iv) the employer of 16- and 17-year-old employees provides notice, and posts a notice, on the scrap paper balers and paper box compactors stating that -

(I) the scrap paper balers and paper box compactors meet the applicable standard described in clause (i);

(II) 16- and 17-year-old employees may only load the scrap paper balers and paper box compactors; and

(III) any employee under the age of 18 may not operate or unload the scrap paper balers and paper box compactors. The Secretary shall publish in the Federal Register a standard that is adopted by the American National Standards Institute for scrap paper balers or paper box compactors and certified by the Secretary to be protective of the safety of minors under clause (i)(II).

(C)

(i) Employers shall prepare and submit to the Secretary reports -

(I) on any injury to an employee under the age of 18 that requires medical treatment (other than first aid) resulting from the employee's contact with a scrap paper baler or paper box compactor during the loading, operation, or unloading of the baler or compactor; and

(II) on any fatality of an employee under the age of 18 resulting from the employee's contact with a scrap paper baler or paper box compactor during the loading, operation, or unloading of the baler or compactor.

(ii) The reports described in clause (i) shall be used by the Secretary to determine whether or not the implementation of subparagraph (A) has had any effect on the safety of children.

(iii) The reports described in clause (i) shall provide -

(I) the name, telephone number, and address of the employer and the address of the place of employment where the incident occurred;

(II) the name, telephone number, and address of the employee who suffered an injury or death as a result of the incident;

(III) the date of the incident;

(IV) a description of the injury and a narrative describing how the incident occurred; and

(V) the name of the manufacturer and the model number of the scrap paper baler or paper box compactor involved in the incident.

(iv) The reports described in clause (i) shall be submitted to the Secretary promptly, but not later than 10 days after the date on which an incident relating to an injury or death occurred.

(v) The Secretary may not rely solely on the reports described in clause (i) as the basis for making a determination that any of the employers described in clause (i) has violated a provision of section 212 of this title relating to oppressive child labor or a regulation or order issued pursuant to section 212 of this title. The Secretary shall, prior to making such a determination, conduct an investigation and inspection in accordance with section 212(b) of this title.

(vi) The reporting requirements of this subparagraph shall expire 2 years after August 6, 1996.

(6) In the administration and enforcement of the child labor provisions of this chapter, employees who are under 17 years of age may not drive automobiles or trucks on public roadways. Employees who are 17 years of age may drive automobiles or trucks on public roadways only if -

(A) such driving is restricted to daylight hours;

(B) the employee holds a State license valid for the type of driving involved in the job performed and has no records of any moving violation at the time of hire;

(C) the employee has successfully completed a State approved driver education course;

(D) the automobile or truck is equipped with a seat belt for the driver and any passengers and the employee's employer has instructed the employee that the seat belts must be used when driving the automobile or truck;

(E) the automobile or truck does not exceed 6,000 pounds of gross vehicle weight;

(F) such driving does not involve -

(i) the towing of vehicles;

(ii) route deliveries or route sales;

(iii) the transportation for hire of property, goods, or passengers; (iv) urgent, time-sensitive deliveries;

(v) more than two trips away from the primary place of employment in any single day for the purpose of delivering goods of the employee's employer to a customer (other than urgent, time-sensitive deliveries);

(vi) more than two trips away from the primary place of employment in any single day for the purpose of transporting passengers (other than employees of the employer);

(vii) transporting more than three passengers (including employees of the employer); or

(viii) driving beyond a 30 mile radius from the employee's place of employment; and

(G) such driving is only occasional and incidental to the employee's employment. For purposes of subparagraph (G), the term "occasional and incidental" is no more than one-third of an employee's worktime in any workday and no more than 20 percent of an employee's worktime in any workweek.

(d) Delivery of newspapers and wreathmaking

The provisions of sections 206, 207, and 212 of this title shall not apply with respect to any employee engaged in the delivery of newspapers to the consumer or to any homeworker engaged in the making of wreaths composed principally of natural holly, pine, cedar, or other evergreens (including the harvesting of the evergreens or other forest products used in making such wreaths).

(e) Maximum hour requirements and minimum wage employees

The provisions of section 207 of this title shall not apply with respect to employees for whom the Secretary of Labor is authorized to establish minimum wage rates as provided in section 206(a)(3) of this title, except with respect to employees for whom such rates are in effect; and with respect to such employees the Secretary may make rules and regulations providing reasonable limitations and allowing reasonable variations, tolerances, and exemptions to and from any or all of the provisions of section 207 of this title if he shall find, after a public hearing on the matter, and taking into account the factors set forth in section 206(a)(3) of this title, that economic conditions warrant such action.

APPENDIX B: INTERNATIONAL LABOR ORGANIZATION CONVENTION 182 AND RECOMMENDATIONS

ILO Convention No. 182
Convention concerning the Prohibition and Immediate Action for the Elimination of the Worst Forms of Child Labour

C. 182 Worst Forms of Child Labour Convention, 1999

The General Conference of the International Labour Organization,

Having been convened at Geneva by the Governing Body of the International Labour Office, and having met in its 87th Session on 1 June 1999, and

Considering the need to adopt new instruments for the prohibition and elimination of the worst forms of child labour, as the main priority for national and international action, including international cooperation and assistance, to complement the Convention and the Recommendation concerning Minimum Age for Admission to Employment, 1973, which remain fundamental instruments on child labour, and

Considering that the effective elimination of the worst forms of child labour requires immediate and comprehensive action, taking into account the importance of free basic education and the need to remove the children concerned from all such work and to provide for their rehabilitation and social integration while addressing the needs of their families, and

Recalling the resolution concerning the elimination of child labour adopted by the International Labour Conference at its 83rd Session in 1996, and

Recognizing that child labour is to a great extent caused by poverty and that the long-term solution lies in sustained economic growth leading to social progress, in particular poverty alleviation and universal education, and

Recalling the Convention on the Rights of the Child adopted by the United Nations General Assembly on 20 November 1989, and

Recalling the ILO Declaration on Fundamental Principles and Rights at Work and its Follow-up, adopted by the International Labour Conference at its 86th Session in 1998, and

Recalling that some of the worst forms of child labour are covered by other international instruments, in particular the Forced Labour Convention, 1930, and the United Nations Supplementary Convention on the Abolition of Slavery, the Slave Trade, and Institutions and Practices Similar to Slavery, 1956, and

Having decided upon the adoption of certain proposals with regard to child labour, which is the fourth item on the agenda of the session, and

Having determined that these proposals shall take the form of an international Convention;

adopts this seventeenth day of June of the year one thousand nine hundred and ninety-nine the following Convention, which may be cited as the Worst Forms of Child Labour Convention, 1999.

Article 1

Each Member which ratifies this Convention shall take immediate and effective measures to secure the prohibition and elimination of the worst forms of child labour as a matter of urgency.

Article 2

For the purposes of this Convention, the term "child" shall apply to all persons under the age of 18.

Article 3

For the purposes of this Convention, the term "the worst forms of child labour" comprises:

(a) all forms of slavery or practices similar to slavery, such as the sale and trafficking of children, debt bondage and serfdom and forced or compulsory labour, including forced or compulsory recruitment of children for use in armed conflict;

(b) the use, procuring or offering of a child for prostitution, for the production of pornography or for pornographic performances;

(c) the use, procuring or offering of a child for illicit activities, in particular for the production and trafficking of drugs as defined in the relevant international treaties;

(d) work which, by its nature or the circumstances in which it is carried out, is likely to harm the health, safety or morals of children.

Article 4

1. The types of work referred to under Article 3(d) shall be determined by national laws or regulations or by the competent authority, after consultation with the organizations of employers and workers concerned, taking into consideration relevant international standards, in particular Paragraphs 3 and 4 of the Worst Forms of Child Labour Recommendation, 1999.

2. The competent authority, after consultation with the organizations of employers and workers concerned, shall identify where the types of work so determined exist.

3. The list of the types of work determined under paragraph 1 of this Article shall be periodically examined and revised as necessary, in consultation with the organizations of employers and workers concerned.

Article 5

Each Member shall, after consultation with employers' and workers' organizations, establish or designate appropriate mechanisms to monitor the implementation of the provisions giving effect to this Convention.

Article 6

1. Each Member shall design and implement programmes of action to eliminate as a priority the worst forms of child labour.

2. Such programmes of action shall be designed and implemented in consultation with relevant government institutions and employers' and workers' organizations, taking into consideration the views of other concerned groups as appropriate.

Article 7

1. Each Member shall take all necessary measures to ensure the effective implementation and enforcement of the provisions giving effect to this Convention including the provision and application of penal sanctions or, as appropriate, other sanctions.

2. Each Member shall, taking into account the importance of education in eliminating child labour, take effective and time-bound measures to:

(a) prevent the engagement of children in the worst forms of child labour;
(b) provide the necessary and appropriate direct assistance for the removal of children from the worst forms of child labour and for their rehabilitation and social integration;
(c) ensure access to free basic education, and, wherever possible and appropriate, vocational training, for all children removed from the worst forms of child labour;
(d) identify and reach out to children at special risk; and
(e) take account of the special situation of girls.

3. Each Member shall designate the competent authority responsible for the implementation of the provisions giving effect to this Convention.

Article 8

Members shall take appropriate steps to assist one another in giving effect to the provisions of this Convention through enhanced international cooperation and/or assistance including support for social and economic development, poverty eradication programmes and universal education.

Article 9

The formal ratifications of this Convention shall be communicated to the Director-General of the International Labour Office for registration.

Article 10

1. This Convention shall be binding only upon those Members of the International Labour Organization whose ratifications have been registered with the Director-General of the International Labour Office.

2. It shall come into force 12 months after the date on which the ratifications of two Members have been registered with the Director General.

3. Thereafter, this Convention shall come into force for any Member 12 months after the date on which its ratification has been registered.

Article 11

1. A Member which has ratified this Convention may denounce it after the expiration of ten years from the date on which the Convention first comes into force, by an act communicated to the Director-General of the International Labour Office for registration. Such denunciation shall not take effect until one year after the date on which it is registered.

2. Each Member which has ratified this Convention and which does not, within the year following the expiration of the period of ten years mentioned in the preceding paragraph, exercise the right of denunciation provided for in this Article, will be bound for another period of ten years and, thereafter, may denounce this Convention at the expiration of each period of ten years under the terms provided for in this Article.

Article 12

1. The Director-General of the International Labour Office shall notify all Members of the International Labour Organization of the registration of all ratifications and acts of denunciation communicated by the Members of the Organization.

2. When notifying the Members of the Organization of the registration of the second ratification, the Director-General shall draw the attention of the Members of the Organization to the date upon which the Convention shall come into force.

Article 13

The Director-General of the International Labour Office shall communicate to the Secretary-General of the United Nations, for registration in accordance with article 102 of the Charter of the United Nations, full particulars of all ratifications and acts of denunciation registered by the Director-General in accordance with the provisions of the preceding Articles.

Article 14

At such times as it may consider necessary, the Governing Body of the International Labour Office shall present to the General Conference a report on the working of this Convention and shall examine the desirability of placing on the agenda of the Conference the question of its revision in whole or in part.

Article 15

1. Should the Conference adopt a new Convention revising this Convention in whole or in part, then, unless the new Convention otherwise provides --

(a) the ratification by a Member of the new revising Convention shall ipso jure involve the immediate denunciation of this Convention, notwithstanding the provisions of Article 11 above, if and when the new revising Convention shall have come into force;

(b) as from the date when the new revising Convention comes into force, this Convention shall cease to be open to ratification by the Members.

2. This Convention shall in any case remain in force in its actual form and content for those Members which have ratified it but have not ratified the revising Convention.

Article 16

The English and French versions of the text of this Convention are equally authoritative.

The foregoing is the authentic text of the Convention unanimously adopted by the General Conference of the International Labour Organization during its Eighty-seventh Session which was held at Geneva and declared closed on 17 June 1999.

IN FAITH WHEREOF we have appended our signatures this day of June 1999.
The President of the Conference,
The Director-General of the International Labour Office

RECOMMENDATION 190
International Labour Conference, 87th Session, Geneva, June 1999

RECOMMENDATION CONCERNING THE PROHIBITION
AND IMMEDIATE ACTION FOR THE ELIMINATION OF THE WORST
FORMS OF CHILD LABOUR
ADOPTED BY THE CONFERENCE AT ITS EIGHTY-SEVENTH SESSION,
GENEVA, 17 JUNE 1999

The General Conference of the International Labour Organization,

Having been convened at Geneva by the Governing Body of the International Labour Office, and having met in its 87th Session on 1 June 1999, and

Having adopted the Worst Forms of Child Labour Convention, 1999, and

Having decided upon the adoption of certain proposals with regard to child labour, which is the fourth item on the agenda of the session, and

Having determined that these proposals shall take the form of a Recommendation supplementing the Worst Forms of Child Labour Convention, 1999; adopts this seventeenth day of June of the year one thousand nine hundred and ninety-nine the following Recommendation, which may be cited as the Worst Forms of Child Labour Recommendation, 1999.

1. The provisions of this Recommendation supplement those of the Worst Forms of Child Labour Convention, 1999 (hereafter referred to as "the Convention"), and should be applied in conjunction with them.

I. Programmes of action

2. The programmes of action referred to in Article 6 of the Convention should be designed and implemented as a matter of urgency, in consultation with relevant government institutions and employers' and workers' organizations, taking into consideration the views of the children directly affected by the worst forms of child labour, their families and, as appropriate, other concerned groups committed to the aims of the Convention and this Recommendation. Such programmes should aim at, inter alia:

(a) identifying and denouncing the worst forms of child labour;

(b) preventing the engagement of children in or removing them from the worst forms of child labour, protecting them from reprisals and providing for their rehabilitation and social integration through measures which address their educational, physical and psychological needs;

(c) giving special attention to:

    (i) younger children;
    (ii) the girl child;
    (iii) the problem of hidden work situations, in which girls are at special risk;
    (iv) other groups of children with special vulnerabilities or needs;

(d) identifying, reaching out to and working with communities where children are at special risk;

(e) informing, sensitizing and mobilizing public opinion and concerned groups, including children and their families.

II. Hazardous work

3. In determining the types of work referred to under Article 3(d) of the Convention, and in identifying where they exist, consideration should be given, inter alia, to:

(a) work which exposes children to physical, psychological or sexual abuse;

(b) work underground, under water, at dangerous heights or in confined spaces;

(c) work with dangerous machinery, equipment and tools, or which involves the manual handling or transport of heavy loads;

(d) work in an unhealthy environment which may, for example, expose children to hazardous substances, agents or processes, or to temperatures, noise levels, or vibrations damaging to their health;

(e) work under particularly difficult conditions such as work for long hours or during the night or work where the child is unreasonably confined to the premises of the employer.

4. For the types of work referred to under Article 3(d) of the Convention and Paragraph 3 above, national laws or regulations or the competent authority could, after consultation with the workers' and employers' organizations concerned, authorize employment or work as from the age of 16 on condition that the health, safety and morals of the children concerned are fully protected, and that the children have received adequate specific instruction or vocational training in the relevant branch of activity.

III. Implementation

5. (1) Detailed information and statistical data on the nature and extent of child labour should be compiled and kept up to date to serve as a basis for determining priorities for national action for the abolition of child labour, in particular for the prohibition and elimination of its worst forms as a matter of urgency.

(2) As far as possible, such information and statistical data should include data disaggregated by sex, age group, occupation, branch of economic activity, status in employment, school attendance and geographical location. The importance of an effective system of birth registration, including the issuing of birth certificates, should be taken into account.

(3) Relevant data concerning violations of national provisions for the prohibition and elimination of the worst forms of child labour should be compiled and kept up to date.

6. The compilation and processing of the information and data referred to in Paragraph 5 above should be carried out with due regard for the right to privacy.

7. The information compiled under Paragraph 5 above should be communicated to the International Labour Office on a regular basis.

8. Members should establish or designate appropriate national mechanisms to monitor the implementation of national provisions for the prohibition and elimination of the worst forms of child labour, after consultation with employers' and workers' organizations.

9. Members should ensure that the competent authorities which have responsibilities for implementing national provisions for the prohibition and

elimination of the worst forms of child labour cooperate with each other and coordinate their activities.

10. National laws or regulations or the competent authority should determine the persons to be held responsible in the event of non-compliance with national provisions for the prohibition and elimination of the worst forms of child labour.

11. Members should, in so far as it is compatible with national law, cooperate with international efforts aimed at the prohibition and elimination of the worst forms of child labour as a matter of urgency by:

(a) gathering and exchanging information concerning criminal offences, including those involving international networks;

(b) detecting and prosecuting those involved in the sale and trafficking of children, or in the use, procuring or offering of children for illicit activities, for prostitution, for the production of pornography or for pornographic performances;

(c) registering perpetrators of such offences.

12. Members should provide that the following worst forms of child labour are criminal offences:

(a) all forms of slavery or practices similar to slavery, such as the sale and trafficking of children, debt bondage and serfdom and forced or compulsory labour, including forced or compulsory recruitment of children for use in armed conflict;

(b) the use, procuring or offering of a child for prostitution, for the production of pornography or for pornographic performances; and

(c) the use, procuring or offering of a child for illicit activities, in particular for the production and trafficking of drugs as defined in the relevant international treaties, or for activities which involve the unlawful carrying or use of firearms or other weapons.

13. Members should ensure that penalties including, where appropriate, criminal penalties are applied for violations of the national provisions for the prohibition

and elimination of any type of work referred to in Article 3(d) of the Convention.

14. Members should also provide as a matter of urgency for other criminal, civil or administrative remedies, where appropriate, to ensure the effective enforcement of national provisions for the prohibition and elimination of the worst forms of child labour, such as special supervision of enterprises which have used the worst forms of child labour, and, in cases of persistent violation, consideration of temporary or permanent revoking of permits to operate.

15. Other measures aimed at the prohibition and elimination of the worst forms of child labour might include the following:

(a) informing, sensitizing and mobilizing the general public, including national and local political leaders, parliamentarians and the judiciary;

(b) involving and training employers' and workers' organizations and civic organizations;

(c) providing appropriate training for the government officials concerned, especially inspectors and law enforcement officials, and for other relevant professionals;

(d) providing for the prosecution in their own country of the Member's nationals who commit offences under its national provisions for the prohibition and immediate elimination of the worst forms of child labour even when these offences are committed in another country;

(e) simplifying legal and administrative procedures and ensuring that they are appropriate and prompt;

(f) encouraging the development of policies by undertakings to promote the aims of the Convention;

(g) monitoring and giving publicity to best practices on the elimination of child labour;

(h) giving publicity to legal or other provisions on child labour in the different languages or dialects;

(i) establishing special complaints procedures and making provisions to protect from discrimination and reprisals those who legitimately expose violations of the provisions of the Convention, as well as establishing helplines or points of contact and ombudspersons;

(j) adopting appropriate measures to improve the educational infrastructure and the training of teachers to meet the needs of boys and girls;

(k) as far as possible, taking into account in national programmes of action:

(i) the need for job creation and vocational training for the parents and adults in the families of children working in the conditions covered by the Convention; and

(ii) the need for sensitizing parents to the problem of children working in such conditions.

16. Enhanced international cooperation and/or assistance among Members for the prohibition and effective elimination of the worst forms of child labour should complement national efforts and may, as appropriate, be developed and implemented in consultation with employers' and workers' organizations. Such international cooperation and/or assistance should include:

(a) mobilizing resources for national or international programmes;

(b) mutual legal assistance;

(c) technical assistance including the exchange of information;

(d) support for social and economic development, poverty eradication programmes and universal education.

The foregoing is the authentic text of the Recommendation unanimously adopted by the General Conference of the International Labour Organization during its Eighty-seventh Session which was held at Geneva and declared closed on 17 June 1999.
IN FAITH WHEREOF we have appended our signatures this day of June 1999.
The President of the Conference,
The Director-General of the International Labour Office

APPENDIX C: EXCERPTS FROM THE CONVENTION ON THE RIGHTS OF THE CHILD

UN Convention on the Rights of the Child, G.A. res. 44/25, annex, 44 U.N. GAOR Supp. (No. 49) at 167, U.N. Doc. A/44/49 (1989).

PREAMBLE

The States Parties to the present Convention,

Considering that, in accordance with the principles proclaimed in the Charter of the United Nations, recognition of the inherent dignity and of the equal and inalienable rights of all members of the human family is the foundation of freedom, justice and peace in the world,

Bearing in mind that the peoples of the United Nations have, in the Charter, reaffirmed their faith in fundamental human rights and in the dignity and worth of the human person, and have determined to promote social progress and better standards of life in larger freedom,

Recognizing that the United Nations has, in the Universal Declaration of Human Rights and in the International Covenants on Human Rights, proclaimed and agreed that everyone is entitled to all the rights and freedoms set forth therein, without distinction of any kind, such as race, colour, sex, language, religion, political or other opinion, national or social origin, property, birth or other status,

Recalling that, in the Universal Declaration of Human Rights, the United Nations has proclaimed that childhood is entitled to special care and assistance,

Convinced that the family, as the fundamental group of society and the natural environment for the growth and well-being of all its members and particularly children, should be afforded the necessary protection and assistance so that it can fully assume its responsibilities within the community,

Recognizing that the child, for the full and harmonious development of his or her personality, should grow up in a family environment, in an atmosphere of happiness, love and understanding,

Considering that the child should be fully prepared to live an individual life in society, and brought up in the spirit of the ideals proclaimed in the Charter of

100

the United Nations, and in particular in the spirit of peace, dignity, tolerance, freedom, equality and solidarity,

Bearing in mind that the need to extend particular care to the child has been stated in the Geneva Declaration of the Rights of the Child of 1924 and in the Declaration of the Rights of the Child adopted by the General Assembly on 20 November 1959 and recognized in the Universal Declaration of Human Rights, in the International Covenant on Civil and Political Rights (in particular in articles 23 and 24), in the International Covenant on Economic, Social and Cultural Rights (in particular in article 10) and in the statutes and relevant instruments of specialized agencies and international organizations concerned with the welfare of children, '

Bearing in mind that, as indicated in the Declaration of the Rights of the Child, "the child, by reason of his physical and mental immaturity, needs special safeguards and care, including appropriate legal protection, before as well as after birth",

Recalling the provisions of the Declaration on Social and Legal Principles relating to the Protection and Welfare of Children, with Special Reference to Foster Placement and Adoption Nationally and Internationally; the United Nations Standard Minimum Rules for the Administration of Juvenile Justice (The Beijing Rules) ; and the Declaration on the Protection of Women and Children in Emergency and Armed Conflict,

Recognizing that, in all countries in the world, there are children living in exceptionally difficult conditions, and that such children need special consideration,

Taking due account of the importance of the traditions and cultural values of each people for the protection and harmonious development of the child,

Recognizing the importance of international co-operation for improving the living conditions of children in every country, in particular in the developing countries,

Have agreed as follows:

PART I
*   *   *

Article 2

1. States Parties shall respect and ensure the rights set forth in the present Convention to each child within their jurisdiction without discrimination of any kind, irrespective of the child's or his or her parent's or legal guardian's race, colour, sex, language, religion, political or other opinion, national, ethnic or social origin, property, disability, birth or other status.

2. States Parties shall take all appropriate measures to ensure that the child is protected against all forms of discrimination or punishment on the basis of the status, activities, expressed opinions, or beliefs of the child's parents, legal guardians, or family members.

Article 3

1. In all actions concerning children, whether undertaken by public or private social welfare institutions, courts of law, administrative authorities or legislative bodies, the best interests of the child shall be a primary consideration.

2. States Parties undertake to ensure the child such protection and care as is necessary for his or her well-being, taking into account the rights and duties of his or her parents, legal guardians, or other individuals legally responsible for him or her, and, to this end, shall take all appropriate legislative and administrative measures.

3. States Parties shall ensure that the institutions, services and facilities responsible for the care or protection of children shall conform with the standards established by competent authorities, particularly in the areas of safety, health, in the number and suitability of their staff, as well as competent supervision.

*   *   *

Article 24

1. States Parties recognize the right of the child to the enjoyment of the highest attainable standard of health and to facilities for the treatment of illness and rehabilitation of health. States Parties shall strive to ensure that no child is deprived of his or her right of access to such health care services.

2. States Parties shall pursue full implementation of this right and, in particular, shall take appropriate measures:

(a) To diminish infant and child mortality;

(b) To ensure the provision of necessary medical assistance and health care to all children with emphasis on the development of primary health care;

(c) To combat disease and malnutrition, including within the framework of primary health care, through, inter alia, the application of readily available technology and through the provision of adequate nutritious foods and clean drinking-water, taking into consideration the dangers and risks of environmental pollution;

(d) To ensure appropriate pre-natal and post-natal health care for mothers;

(e) To ensure that all segments of society, in particular parents and children, are informed, have access to education and are supported in the use of basic knowledge of child health and nutrition, the advantages of breastfeeding, hygiene and environmental sanitation and the prevention of accidents;

(f) To develop preventive health care, guidance for parents and family planning education and services.

3. States Parties shall take all effective and appropriate measures with a view to abolishing traditional practices prejudicial to the health of children.

4. States Parties undertake to promote and encourage international co-operation with a view to achieving progressively the full realization of the right recognized in the present article. In this regard, particular account shall be taken of the needs of developing countries

*   *   *

Article 28

1. States Parties recognize the right of the child to education, and with a view to achieving this right progressively and on the basis of equal opportunity, they shall, in particular:

(a) Make primary education compulsory and available free to all;

(b) Encourage the development of different forms of secondary education, including general and vocational education, make them available and accessible to every child, and take appropriate measures such as the introduction of free education and offering financial assistance in case of need;

(c) Make higher education accessible to all on the basis of capacity by every appropriate means;

(d) Make educational and vocational information and guidance available and accessible to all children;

(e) Take measures to encourage regular attendance at schools and the reduction of drop-out rates.

2. States Parties shall take all appropriate measures to ensure that school discipline is administered in a manner consistent with the child's human dignity and in conformity with the present Convention.

3. States Parties shall promote and encourage international cooperation in matters relating to education, in particular with a view to contributing to the elimination of ignorance and illiteracy throughout the world and facilitating access to scientific and technical knowledge and modern teaching methods. In this regard, particular account shall be taken of the needs of developing countries.

*   *   *

Article 32

1. States Parties recognize the right of the child to be protected from economic exploitation and from performing any work that is likely to be hazardous or to interfere with the child's education, or to be harmful to the child's health or physical, mental, spiritual, moral or social development.

2. States Parties shall take legislative, administrative, social and educational measures to ensure the implementation of the present article. To this end, and having regard to the relevant provisions of other international instruments, States Parties shall in particular:

(a) Provide for a minimum age or minimum ages for admission to employment;

(b) Provide for appropriate regulation of the hours and conditions of employment;

(c) Provide for appropriate penalties or other sanctions to ensure the effective enforcement of the present article.